T0357602

Cambridge Elements ☰

Elements in Archaeological Perspectives on Materials and
Technologies
edited by
A. Mark Pollard
University of Oxford
Chris Gosden
University of Oxford

GLAZED CERAMICS OF THE ISLAMIC WORLD 700–1600 CE

Moujan Matin
University of Toronto
Michael Tite
University of Oxford

CAMBRIDGE
UNIVERSITY PRESS

Shaftesbury Road, Cambridge CB2 8EA, United Kingdom

One Liberty Plaza, 20th Floor, New York, NY 10006, USA

477 Williamstown Road, Port Melbourne, VIC 3207, Australia

314–321, 3rd Floor, Plot 3, Splendor Forum, Jasola District Centre, New Delhi – 110025, India

103 Penang Road, #05–06/07, Visioncrest Commercial, Singapore 238467

Cambridge University Press is part of Cambridge University Press & Assessment, a department of the University of Cambridge.

We share the University's mission to contribute to society through the pursuit of education, learning and research at the highest international levels of excellence.

www.cambridge.org
Information on this title: www.cambridge.org/9781009582902

DOI: 10.1017/9781009582919

First published 2025

A catalogue record for this publication is available from the British Library

ISBN 978-1-009-58290-2 Hardback
ISBN 978-1-009-58289-6 Paperback
ISSN 2754-2939 (online)
ISSN 2754-2920 (print)

Cambridge University Press & Assessment has no responsibility for the persistence or accuracy of URLs for external or third-party internet websites referred to in this publication and does not guarantee that any content on such websites is, or will remain, accurate or appropriate.

For EU product safety concerns, contact us at Calle de José Abascal, 56, 1°, 28003 Madrid, Spain, or email eugpsr@cambridge.org.

Glazed Ceramics of the Islamic World 700–1600 CE

Elements in Archaeological Perspectives on Materials and Technologies

DOI: 10.1017/9781009582919
First published online: April 2025

Moujan Matin
University of Toronto

Michael Tite
University of Oxford

Author for correspondence: Moujan Matin, moujan.matin@uwo.ca

Abstract: Of all the material culture of the Islamic World prior to the sixteenth century, only ceramics survive in a way which forms a continuous representative visual history. As such, ceramics provide a unique collection of material from which to study the history of technology. The main technological developments associated with glazed Islamic ceramics were the introduction of tin-opacified glazes, stonepaste bodies, and an extended range of colorants. For each of these developments, consideration is given to the reasons why new technologies were introduced, from where the ideas for the new technologies originated, and why particular technological choices were made. In addition, brief consideration is given both to the very different glaze technologies employed in contemporary China, and to the subsequent spread of the glazed Islamic technology into Western Europe.

Keywords: ceramics, glazes, technology, innovations, Islam

ISBNs: 9781009582902 (HB), 9781009582896 (PB), 9781009582919 (OC)
ISSNs: 2754-2939 (online), 2754-2920 (print)

Contents

1 Introduction

The glazed ceramics of the Islamic World play a uniquely significant role in understanding the social, economic, and historical dynamics of the region. Prior to the Islamic period, archaeological records show limited evidence of glazed ceramics. However, with the emergence of early Islamic culture, glazed ceramics suddenly become widespread, becoming a diagnostic characteristic of the period in the archaeological records. This shift mirrors the transformative changes in social and economic structures during the Islamic period, and it is in the study of ceramic production that these transformations are reflected.

Of all the material culture of the Islamic World from its beginnings during the seventh century CE through the pre-modern period (i.e., before the sixteenth century), only ceramics survive in a way which forms a continuous representative visual history. The art historical study of Islamic ceramics has largely relied on materials from museum and private collections around the World, affected largely by acquisition choices, fashions in art market, and uncertainties about provenance. Decades of work on these materials have provided connections between these initially isolated types of glazed pottery and contributing to an art historical narrative and developmental sequence as outlined in seminal books by Arthur Lane (1947, 1957a) and Oliver Watson (2004). Since the early twentieth century, archaeological discoveries have enriched this narrative, although the material recovered through excavations has often remained – and to some extent still remains – disconnected from art historical interpretations. Moreover, no major kiln sites have been thoroughly excavated and published, making it difficult to definitively identify the workshops responsible for producing key types of glazed Islamic pottery. Therefore, the names of pottery types associated with the names of Islamic sites as used in art historical literature, such as 'Samarra wares' or 'Raqqa wares' are speculative and do not necessarily indicate the actual production sites of these ceramics.

Another significant challenge in this field is the patchy coverage of knowledge, with certain geographical regions and time periods still being poorly understood. This applies not only regionally but also on a broader scale. For example, we have very limited knowledge of glazed pottery production in Western and Central Iran before the twelfth century, and even after that, our understanding remains incomplete.

The technological study of Islamic pottery has been built upon the existing art historical narrative, inevitably inheriting its gaps and limitations. It has relied on sherds from both museum collections and archaeological sites for chemical analyses, with a greater focus on pottery produced before the sixteenth century. This focus is due to the fact that, after the sixteenth century, intact glazed pottery vessels that survive in good condition above ground – rather than fragments – become more abundant, making them generally unsuitable for destructive analysis. This is also why the chronological scope of this paper ends at the sixteenth century.

As we will explore in the following sections, however, technological studies of Islamic pottery have, in many ways, revised and enriched the 'classic' art historical narrative, providing new lines of evidence and deepening our understanding. These studies have also brought greater focus to the processes of production, the craftspeople involved, and the transfer of techniques. In this book, we aim to present a nuanced perspective on the technological developments in Islamic glazed ceramics, moving beyond a linear or overly simplistic depiction of their evolution. We recognise the significant diversity in raw materials, production methods, and technological trajectories, which varied widely across different regions and time periods. The studies included in this volume reflect a variety of sample sizes, and our interpretations reflect the currently available published data. By synthesising these studies, our goal is not to present a singular or definitive 'truth' but to provide a foundation and direction for future research to build upon.

Where relevant in this paper, we have highlighted the choices made by Islamic potters. It should be noted that, when referring to 'Islamic' potters, it is based solely on the fact that the regions in question were under Islamic rule at the time. This designation does not necessarily reflect the religion or beliefs of the potters themselves.

Technological studies of glazed pottery are facilitated by the fact that, in contrast to metalwork and glass, ceramics were not typically recycled. As a result, one can, uniquely, trace the production technology for Islamic ceramics from the seventh century onwards. This examination of technology is multifaceted, as it encompasses economic aspects, trade patterns and cross-cultural interactions, access to raw materials, all of which, in turn, enrich the study of the social and historical context.

There has been extensive technological study of metalwork over the past hundred years by means of its microstructural examination in polished section in reflected light (Smith 1981). In contrast, comparable studies of ceramics have lagged behind, principally because the optical microscope is of limited use in the study of their very complex and fine-grained microstructures. Some chemical analyses of Islamic glazed ceramics were conducted during the mid-twentieth century, but these were sporadic and without much explanation of the technological aspects (see, e.g., Frierman 1970; Kiefer 1956; Wilkinson 1947). Therefore, the technological study of ancient ceramics, including glazed Islamic ceramics, has been delayed until the development of, and easy access to, Scanning Electron Microscopes (SEM) with attached X-ray fluorescent analytical facilities (XRF) during the 1970s (Tite 1992).

Tite and Maniatis (1975) published one of the earliest papers using SEM to study ceramics, initially focusing on a sequence from Iraq, to estimate firing temperatures and assess physical properties. Their work expanded to include ceramics from the Near East and Central and Southeast Europe, integrating semi-quantitative XRF analyses for lime contents. Additionally, Tite et al. (1982) examined high gloss surface finishes in Greek Attic and Roman Samian wares.

Tite (1988, 1989) further advanced SEM examination techniques, applying them to Chinese and glazed Islamic ceramics, including Iznik wares, in which polished sections replaced fracture surfaces to provide quantitative analyses. Kingery and Vandiver (1986) also made significant contributions, extensively using SEM to investigate the production technology of nine 'ceramic masterpieces' ranging from Song Dynasty (960–1279 CE) Longquan Celadon to Wedgwood Jasperware (eighteenth century CE), and including Kashan lustrewares and Iznik tiles.

Subsequently, Robert Mason, having previously used optical petrography to investigate the centres for the production of Islamic ceramics (Mason and Keall 1990, Mason 1991), completed a DPhil on glazed Islamic ceramics (Mason 1994) at the University of Oxford under the supervision of Professor Michael Tite. This research resulted in published papers on the beginnings of stonepaste technology (Mason and Tite 1994), tin-opacification of glazes (Mason and Tite 1997) and underglaze polychrome ceramics (Mason et al. 2001).

Initially, the styles and technologies of seventh century Islamic ceramics show little difference from those current in the pre-Islamic period. Archaeological ceramic assemblages are dominated by utilitarian wares, with glazed ware being only a small minority. However, towards the end of eighth century, radical changes took place in the Eastern Mediterranean, with the emergence of distinctive Islamic glazed wares and the production of regional fine wares. The earliest phases of glazed Islamic fine wares are represented by Coptic Glazed wares (CGW) first produced in Egypt in late eighth century, and their further development into the Yellow Glazed Family wares (YGF) first produced slightly later in the Levant (Section 3).

From Egypt and the Levant, the glazed Islamic fine wares spread eastwards through Syria, into southern Mesopotamia (i.e., Iraq) and Iran, and beyond into Central Asia (e.g., Nishapur, Samarqand and Uzbekistan) (Sections 3, 4, and 5), as well as into Mughal India which is not discussed in the present paper (see Gill and Rehren 2014, 2017). Subsequently, the Seljuqs spread back from Iran and Central Asia into Anatolia where, in 1453 CE, the Ottoman Empire ultimately conquered and replaced the Byzantine Empire (Section 6).

In addition, glazed Islamic fine-wares spread westwards into al-Andalus (i.e., Spain); and into the coastal area of north Africa from where it spread into Sicily, as well as onto the Swahili coast of east Africa. However, in the present paper, because of its word limit, this westward spread of glazed Islamic ceramics is only considered in sufficient detail needed to explain how the Islamic ceramic technology eventually emerged in Christian western Europe for the production of Italian maiolica and Medici porcelain (Section 7).

The production of glazed Islamic ceramics involved a number of major technological developments, as compared to previously produced Roman and Byzantine glazed ceramics. Perhaps of prime importance was the introduction of tin-opacified glazes (Section 2.1), with yellow lead stannate opacified glazes being used in the production of CGW in Egypt, and white tin oxide (as well as yellow lead stannate) opacified glazes being used in the production of YGF in the Levant. Subsequently, the use of white tin oxide opacified glazes spread throughout the Islamic world and beyond into Europe (Section 7). Yellow lead stannate opacified glazes also spread eastwards from Egypt and the Levant, but were used less extensively. Also, in Egypt, lead antimonate replaced lead stannate as the yellow opacifier by second half of ninth century (Section 4.1.1), and from Egypt, the use of lead antimonate yellow spread across North Africa and into Sicily (Section 7.2), eventually being used as the yellow colorant in the decoration of Italian maiolica (Section 7.3).

The second major Islamic technological development was the introduction of lustre decoration (Section 2.2), which is associated with a layer of silver and copper nanoparticles created just below the surface of the glaze, and which results in a metallic and iridescent appearance. Depending mainly on its Cu/Ag ratio, the lustre tone varies widely from yellow and green to brown and red. The earliest lustreware is found at Samarra in Southern Mesopotamia (Section 3.2.2), from where it spread widely, including to Egypt, Syria, Iran and al-Andalus.

The third major technological development in the production of Islamic ceramics was the introduction of stonepaste bodies (Section 2.3) which were first produced in Egypt during the eleventh century. Subsequently, the use of stonepaste bodies in the production of Islamic fine wares spread to Syria, Iran and beyond. Typically, stonepaste bodies consist of some ten parts crushed quartz, one part crushed glass and one part fine white clay. The result is a hard white body which better imitated the imported Chinese porcelains.

The development of underglaze painting, initially extensively practiced in Iran, Egypt, and Syria, and later spreading to Anatolia and China, marked the final technological development in the production of Islamic ceramics (Section 2.4.3). This technique involves painting directly onto the ceramic body, which is subsequently covered by a transparent glaze and fired. Subsequent to this, changes primarily pertained to stylistic variations rather than technical innovations.

The glaze types used by Islamic potters are principally high lead, as used previously, together with a new lead-alkali glaze type (Section 2.4.1). In addition to lustre decoration, a wide range of other colorants are used in the decoration of Islamic glazes (Section 2.4.2). These include ion-based colorants such as copper blue, turquoise and green (depending on the glaze-type), cobalt dark blue and manganese purple as well as particulate colorants such as lead stannate yellow, tin oxide white, bole red and chromite black.

In the following sections, we will follow the developments of the production technology of Islamic ceramics in different parts of the Islamic world in the period from 700 to 1600 CE. Figures 1 and 2 show the maps with the locations of sites mentioned in the text, and Figure 3 provides a chronological timeline of Islamic dynasties. The period of focus ends at the beginning of the seventeenth century. Iznik wares are the latest group of wares discussed in the text. Persian Safavid wares chronologically overlap with Iznik wares, but they are not included here (see Golombek et al. 2014). The primary method discussed in this paper is the invasive chemical and microstructural analysis of ceramic sherds using Scanning Electron Microscopy (SEM). However, non-invasive techniques, such as Raman spectroscopy and micro-XRF, have also been applied where relevant. While the majority of the analysed fragments are from ceramic vessels, the study of Islamic ceramics saw a significant expansion in the production of ceramic tiles after the Seljuq and Ilkhanid periods. Consequently, a substantial portion of the samples studied from these periods are tiles, including Lajvardina tiles from Iran, and Seljuq, Masters of Tabriz, and Iznik tiles from Anatolia (Sections 5 and 6). Throughout the following Sections we will consider, as appropriate, the following questions relating to the emergence and subsequent development of new technologies:

- How were existing technologies transformed or how was a new technology first invented/discovered?
- Why was the transformed or new technology adopted?
- How was the new technology transferred both geographically (from region to region) and chronologically (from period to period)?
- In adopting a new technology, what technological choices were made and why?

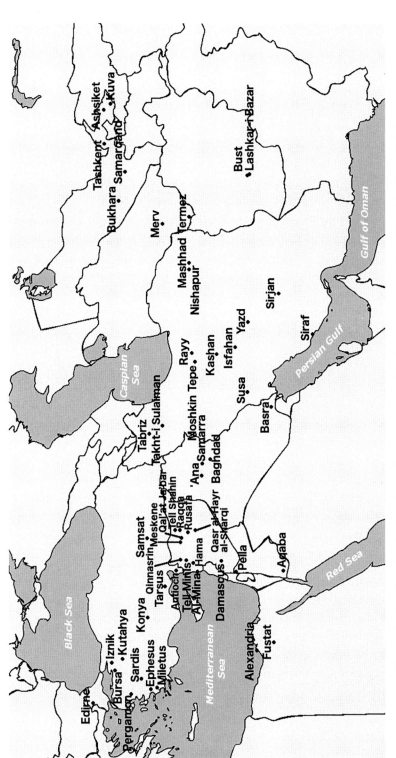

Figure 1 Map showing the locations of sites mentioned in the text spanning from Egypt to Central Asia.

Figure 2 Map showing the locations of sites mentioned in the text within the Western Islamic region.

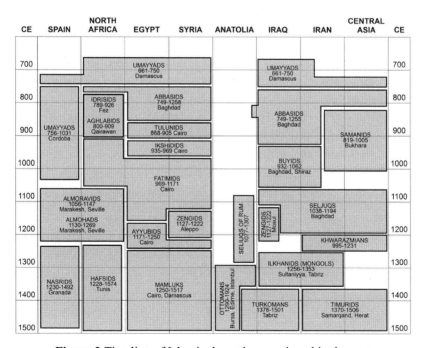

Figure 3 Timeline of Islamic dynasties mentioned in the text.

2 Technological Innovations

The history of Islamic ceramics has witnessed several technological innovations, but four stand out as major technological revolutions: the introduction of tin-based opaque glazing in the eighth century CE (Section 2.1), lusterware production in the ninth century CE (Section 2.2), stonepaste body manufacture in the eleventh century CE (Section 2.3), and underglaze-painted wares during twelfth and thirteenth centuries CE (Section 2.4). The four are the most long-lasting and widespread Islamic, indeed global, technologies, and hence reflect the prevailing social, economic, and political cultures over the *longue durée*. In addition, Islamic potters significantly increased the range of glaze types and their compositions (Section 2.4.1), and the range of glaze colorants (Section 2.4.2), as well as adding, as the fourth major technological innovation, underglaze-painted wares to the glazing methods previously used (Section 2.4.3).

Section 2 examines the science of these four technological innovations, as well as the processes and complexities of their production. Any potential precursors to these four technological innovations are noted, and their possible role in the emergence of these innovations are briefly considered, together with the context of their regional histories and chronologies, and how they developed, changed, and spread across and beyond the Islamic lands. Included in Section 2 are two overview tables, represented as Tables 1 and 2, which summarise the technological data relating to each of the geographical and chronological ceramic groups considered. Table 1 lists the typical compositions of Islamic stonepaste bodies, and Table 2 lists the typical glaze compositions for the Islamic ceramic groups. Included in Table 2 are the glaze compositions for both the transparent high lead and alkali-lime precursors to, and as well as the tin opacified lead-alkali successors to Islamic glazes. The analytical data in Tables 1 and 2 have been normalised to 100 wt%, but no attempt has been made to normalise the analytical ranges, cited from various publications and given in the text.

2.1 Tin-Based Opacification of Ceramic Glazes

Tin-based opacification designates a technique where tin-based crystals, namely lead stannate (i.e., lead-tin-oxide with the formula $Pb(Sn,Si)O_3$) and tin oxide (SnO_2) were used to produce, respectively, yellow and white opaque glass and opaque ceramic glazes (Figures 4 and 5) (Molera et al. 1999; Matin 2019). The glaze opacity is produced by the interaction between the tin-based crystals that are dispersed in a glaze matrix and the incident light, which results in the reflection and scattering of light (Vendrell et al. 2007). The resulting opaque glazes were significant in that, when applied over the entire surface of ceramics,

Table 1 Table showing summary of stonepaste body compositions (normalised to 100%).

Section	Sample number	SiO$_2$	Al$_2$O$_3$	Na$_2$O	K$_2$O	CaO	MgO	FeO	PbO	Reference
Fatimid (960–1160 CE)										
	Egypt Fustat – Fu.P24*	65.4	12.7	5.7	1.4	11.2	0.4	2.5	0.7	Mason & Tite 1994
	Egypt Fustat – average	87.7	3.2	3.2	0.3	2.9	0.3	1.3	1.0	Tite et al. 2011
	Egypt Fustat – A/B/FGrp1 (medium vitrification)	85.9	4.5	2.4	1.0	3.5	0.4	1.5	0.7	Matin & Ownby 2023
	Egypt Fustat – DGrp2 (high vitrification)	86.4	4.4	2.2	0.9	3.7	0.4	1.4	0.5	Matin & Ownby 2023
	Egypt Fustat – EGrp2 (high vitrification)	86.4	4.3	2.3	0.6	4.9	0.4	1.1	bd	Matin & Ownby 2023
	Egypt Fustat – CGrp2 (very high vitrification)	85.2	4.5	2.0	0.7	4.9	0.4	1.3	0.9	Matin & Ownby 2023
	Syria Tell Minis – 521 800	84.2	5.2	2.9	1.9	3.6	0.9	1.3	na	Tonghini 1998: 91
	Syria Raqqa – 61f 832	86.6	3.7	2.3	1.1	3.3	1.9	1.1	na	Tonghini 1998: 91
Seljuq (1050–1200 CE)										
	Iran Moshkin Tepe – Grp I 18–2–75	77.7	12.7	3.9	2.5	1.6	0.8	0.7	na	Matin 2022
	Iran Moshkin Tepe – Grp II 18–2–74 (more extensive vitrification)	74.5	12.7	4.7	3.1	2.5	1.5	0.9	na	Matin 2022

Table 1 (cont.)

Section	Sample number	SiO$_2$	Al$_2$O$_3$	Na$_2$O	K$_2$O	CaO	MgO	FeO	PbO	Reference
	Iran Kashan (lustre, mina'i, and lajvardina wares)-average	85.2	6.5	3.5	1.5	1.6	0.6	0.6	0.5	Kingery and Vandiver 1986; Mason 2004; Osete-Cortina et al. 2010; Tite et al. 2011
Ilkhanid (1256–1335 CE)										
	Iran (UGP)-average	90.2	1.1	2.4	0.9	2.8	1.6	1.0	bd	Mason 2004
	Iran Jahan-Nama (UGP)-JN-7	72.9	20.1	3.3	0.8	1.1	1.5	0.3	na	Aarab et al. 2025
Mamluk (1250–1350 CE)										
	Egypt Fustat (UGP) – average	90.0	2.0	1.2	0.4	4.5	1.1	0.8	bd	Tite et al. 2011
	Egypt 741 888	84.6	1.5	2.1	0.8	7.8	2.5	0.7	na	Tonghini 1998: 91
	Syria Damascus (UGP) – average	89.8	1.6	1.2	0.4	5.5	1.2	0.3	bd	Tite et al. 2011
Timurid (1400–1440 CE)										
	Iran Nishapur (UGBP) – average	92.3	3.1	1.6	0.4	1.5	0.5	0.6	bd	Mason 1996; Tite et al. 2011
Ottoman (1480–1700 CE)										
	Turkey Iznik – average	90.6	2.5	1.8	0.2	2.1	0.8	0.7	bd	Mason 1996; Tite et al. 2011
	Italy Medici porcelain – BM Cat. 248	76.4	9.4	4.7	4.5	2.9	1.1	0.5	0.4	Tite 1991

*bd: below detection; na: not analysed; UGP: underglaze painting; UGBP: Underglaze blue painting; * proto-stonepaste*

Table 2 Table showing summary of glaze compositions (normalised to 100%).

Section	Sample number	Glaze type	SiO$_2$	PbO	SnO$_2$	Na$_2$O	K$_2$O	CaO +MgO	Al$_2$O$_3$	MnO	FeO	TiO$_2$	Sb$_2$O$_3$	Pb/Sn	Reference
Yellow – lead-tin-oxide opacified glazes															
4	Syria – Raqqa 11	High lead	28.8	67.4	1.9	bd	bd	0.3	1.5	bd	bd	bd		41.4	Matin et al. 2018
4	Egypt – Fustat 1	High lead	27.8	65.4	2.7	0.2	bd	0.3	2.9	0.1	0.6	bd		28.5	Matin et al. 2018
4	Iran – Susa 1	High lead	27.9	62.3	3.3	0.6	1.4	2.4	1.0	0.2	0.5	0.4		22.2	Matin et al. 2018
7	Andulucia – Madinat al-Zahra MZ2	High lead	24.5	64.7	5.9	0.2	0.5	2.7	1.2	na	0.3	na		12.9	Salinas et al. 2019
5	Iran Nishapur– Buffware ROM.20	High lead	35.4	60.0	1.1	1.5	0.9	0.7	na	na	0.3	na		63.2	Mason 2004
5	Iran Nishapur-Opaque yellow glazed wares Nishapur9	High lead	26.8	65.4	4.7	0.4	0.1	1.2	0.8	bd	0.6	bd		16.4	Matin et al. 2018
5	Iran Takht-i Suleiman – Takht.6	High lead	30.9	63.0	4.2	0.4	0.5	0.3	0.7	bd	bd	bd		17.7	Matin et al. 2018
5	Turkmenistan Merv-Merv.1	High lead	27.6	65.8	3.1	0.2	0.5	1.1	1.1	0.2	0.3	0.1		25.0	Matin et al. 2018
Yellow – lead-antimonate opacified glazes															
7	Sicily – Palermo PM 65	High lead	29.5	60.6	1.9	0.4	0.3	0.2	bd	bd	1.4	bd	5.6		Testolini 2018: 194
4	Egypt – Fustat ALX 152	Lead-alkali	34.5	57.2	0.3	1.7	1.5	1.9	1.5	bd	0.5	bd	0.9		Salinas et al. 2019
White – tin opacified glazes															
7	Sicily – Palermo PM 65	High lead	32.4	60.8	4.7	0.6	0.3	0.2	bd	na	0.9	bd		15.3	Testolini 2018: 194
5	Uzbekistan Samarqand – Opaque white glazed ware – Samarqand6	Lead-alkali	56.0	18.9	6.1	6.5	3.0	5.5	3.6	bd	0.4	bd		3.7	Matin et al. 2018
6	Anatolia Beylik – Turquoise B2Y66	Lead-alkali	35.6	44.8	6.9	7.4	0.4	3.4	1.1	bd	0.3	na		7.7	Burlot & Waksman 2021
4	Syria – Raqqa 3	Lead-alkali	40.1	43.6	7.2	2.4	1.4	4.1	0.8	0.1	0.4	bd		7.1	Matin et al. 2018
7	Andulucia – Cordoba PAL15	Lead-alkali	41.7	39.0	6.8	2.6	2.1	3.6	3.0	0.2	0.9	bd		6.8	Salinas & Pradell 2020
4	Egypt – Fustat lustre P144	Lead-alkali	59.9	24.9	9.3	2.1	1.6	1.2	1.0	na	bd	na		3.2	Mason & Tite 1997
6	Anatolia Seljuq– Turquoise 3-G	Lead-alkali	53.1	15.9	5.2	13.5	1.3	3.8	5.1	bd	2.0	0.2		3.6	Öztürk et al. 2022

Table 2 (cont.)

Section	Sample number	Glaze type	SiO$_2$	PbO	SnO$_2$	Na$_2$O	K$_2$O	CaO +MgO	Al$_2$O$_3$	MnO	FeO	TiO$_2$	Sb$_2$O$_3$	Pb/Sn	Reference
5	Iran Kashan Seljuq/Ilkhanid– Lustre P10326	Lead-alkali	56.1	22.4	3.9	6.8	2.1	6.6	1.8	bd	0.3	0.2		6.8	Pradell et al. 2008
5	Iran Kashan Seljuq– Mina'i ROM.07	Lead-alkali	53.4	21.6	10.0	7.3	1.5	4.3	1.4	na	0.5	na		2.5	Mason et al. 2001
5	Iran Ilkhanid– Lajvardina C17VO (blue)	Lead-alkali	58.5	15.6	5.5	8.7	1.5	7.0	1.8	na	1.5	bd		3.4	Osete-Cortina et al. 2010
3	Iran – Susa 19	Alkali-lead	68.3	4.7	5.2	5.5	4.8	8.9	1.4	0.4	0.7	0.1		1.1	Matin et al. 2018
3	Mesopotamia – Samarra 6	Alkali-lead	70.3	4.3	2.2	6.9	5.0	8.3	1.9	0.4	0.6	0.1		2.3	Matin et al. 2018
7	Italian Archaic maiolica – 13th century CE	High lead	30.8	44.2	21.4	0.1	0.2	1.7	1.2	na	0.4	bd		2.4	Tite 2009
7	Italian Renaissance maiolica – 15th century CE	Lead-alkali	60.6	18.4	5.1	bd	5.8	3.9	4.5	na	1.8	na		4.3	Tite 2009
	Transparent glazes – High lead and Lead-alkali														
2	Roman – 1st century–4th century CE	High lead	17.5	71.1	na	0.2	0.8	0.8	8.7	na	0.8	na			Walton & Tite 2010
2	Byzantine – 13th century CE	High lead	21.0	70.5	na	bd	0.2	0.8	6.9	na	0.5	na			Armstrong et al. 1997
7	Tunisia – Bir Ftouha T1	High lead	30.1	62.6	bd	0.4	1.1	1.4	3.1	bd	1.1	0.2			Salinas et al. 2020
5	Southern Kazakhstan – SP Mean	High lead	37.9	54.4	0.0	0.3	0.9	1.7	3.2	0.3	1.2	0.1			Klesner et al. 2021
5	Uzbekistan Termez – SP TA10	High lead	36.8	55.7	bd	0.8	0.5	1.7	2.0	0.8	1.7	na			Molera et al. 2020
5	Uzbekistan Ashsiket – SP Average	High lead	40.3	53.8	na	0.3	1.3	0.9	3.0	na	0.4	na			Henshaw 2010
5	Afghanistan Bust and Lashkar-i Bazar– SP	High lead	33.8	57.6	bd	0.8	0.7	3.0	2.9	na	1.2	na			Gulmini et al. 2013
6	Anatolia Beylik B2N70	High lead	31.6	62.1	bd	0.7	bd	0.8	2.3	2.3	0.3	na			Burlot & Waksman 2021
6	Anatolia Iznik – Benaki 42	Lead-alkali	58.3	29.2	5.1	4.8	0.9	0.9	0.4	na	0.4	bd			Paynter et al. 2004
4	Syria Tell Minis – 46g 220	Lead-alkali	54.9	28.1	bd	9.3	0.9	4.6	1.4	bd	0.8	na			Tonghini 1998: 90
4	Syria Polychrome relief MRT31	Lead-alkali	60.0	22.1	bd	9.5	1.5	4.8	1.5	na	0.6	na			Mason et al. 2001
6	Anatolia Miletus BYZ284	Lead-alkali	65.4	15.3	bd	13.1	1.7	1.8	2.2	bd	0.6	na			Burlot et al. 2020

Transparent glazes – Alkali-lime

2	Egyptian faience – 2nd millennium BCE	Alkali-lime	72.9	na	na	18.1	2.5	5.2	0.8	na	0.5	na	Tite et al. 1983
2	Nuzi – 4th century BCE	Alkali-lime	69.1	na	na	13.4	5.8	10.6	0.7	na	0.4	na	Tite & Shortland 2008
2	Parthian – c.250 BCE-220 CE	Alkali-lime	63.2	na	na	14.6	4.9	9.8	3.3	na	4.1	na	Tite & Shortland 2008
4	Syria Raqqa – 66j 717	Alkali-lime	70.4	bd	bd	18.1	1.2	6.8	2.2	bd	1.3	na	Tonghini 1998: 90
4	Egypt Mamluk – 73k 131	Alkali-lime	65.5	bd	bd	17.1	3.4	12.0	1.2	bd	0.9	na	Tonghini 1998: 90
4	Syria – UGP ASH 33	Alkali-lime	73.7	bd	bd	17.0	2.4	6.3	0.4	na	0.2	na	Mason et al. 2001
5	Iran Seljuq Moshkin Tepe – Mono 18-2-75 (turquoise)	Alkali-lime	69.2	bd	bd	11.9	3.1	12.6	2.0	bd	0.8	0.3	Matin 2020
5	Iran Seljuq – Silhouette MDT02	Alkali-lime	68.5	0.1	bd	14.5	2.2	10.6	2.9	na	1.1	na	Mason et al. 2001
5	Iran Seljuq – UGP ASH 51	Alkali-lime	69.9	bd	bd	14.9	2.1	10.9	1.4	na	0.8	na	Mason et al. 2001
5	Iran Ilkhanid Jahan-Nama – UGP JN-7	Alkali-lime	62.9	bd	0.1	22.3	1.6	8.7	4.1	na	0.3	na	Aarab et al. 2025
5	Iran Ilkhanid – Lajvardina Rayy	Alkali-lime	69.0	0.6	0.3	12.3	3.3	10.5	2.3	0.1	1.5	0.1	Holakooei et al. 2023
5	Iran Kashan Seljuq/Ilkhanid – Lustre RYY11	Alkali-lime	73.7	bd	na	15.7	2.7	5.4	1.5	na	1.0	na	Mason 2004
6	Anatolia Seljuq 6-J	Alkali-lime	68.3	0.5	bd	10.8	2.5	6.8	5.7	3.1	2.1	0.2	Öztürk et al. 2022

bd: below detection; na: not analysed; UGP: underglaze painting; SP: Slip painting; Mono: Monochrome stonepaste

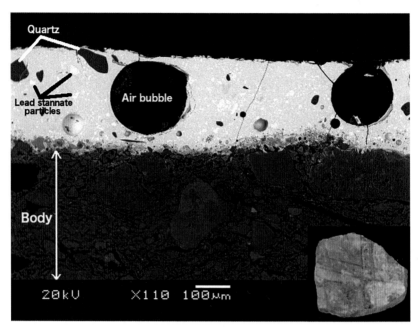

Figure 4 Backscattered SEM photomicrograph of a section through opaque yellow glaze into the body of a Yellow Glazed Family (YGF) sherd from Al-Mina. Yellow glaze showing a scatter of lead-stannate particles (white), air bubbles, and undissolved quartz particles (Victoria and Albert Museum, acc. no. C242 J-1937).

they completely disguised the ceramic bodies and provided a smooth background onto which decorations could be applied. Such glazing technique radically revolutionised the production of ceramics in the Islamic lands and subsequently in Europe.

The use of tin-based opacifiers was preceded by that of antimony-based opacifiers (i.e., lead antimonate yellow and calcium antimonate white), which were first used in Egypt and the Near East in the production of opaque glasses in the mid second millennium BCE and then continued in use until about the fourth century CE (Turner and Rooksby 1961: 3–5). However, in the fourth century CE, the Roman and Byzantine worlds switched to lead stannate and tin oxide for the production of opaque glasses, most commonly used in mosaic tesserae (for a review see Matin 2019). At the same time as the switch in glass opacifiers, glassmakers also switched from antimony to manganese as the decolorant used to counter the effect of small quantities of iron impurities in the glass. Recently, Degryse et al. (2024) have used lead and re-evaluated antimony isotope analyses to show that the most likely source of stibnite (Sb_2S_3) for late Roman

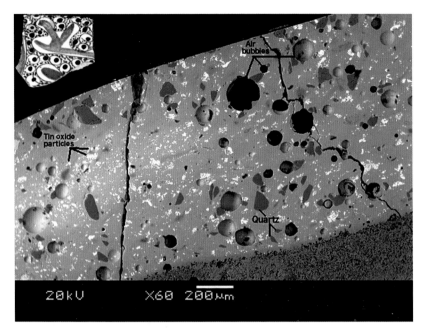

Figure 5 Backscattered SEM photomicrograph of a section through opaque white glaze into the body of a lustre-painted sherd from Samarra. White glaze showing a scatter of tin oxide particles (white), air bubbles, and quartz/feldspar particles. (Victoria and Albert Museum, acc. no. C.769–1923).

decoloured natron glass was the mines of Dacia in Romania. Therefore, the switch to manganese as the glass decolorant occurred at the time that Dacia was lost to the Roman Empire. Although, because of its high lead content, it is not possible to prove that the stibnite used to produce lead antimonate yellow came from Dacia, the fact that the switch in opacifier and decolorant occurred at more-or-less the same time makes this probable.

Around the time of the arrival of Islam in the Eastern Mediterranean in the eighth century CE, potters adapted the Roman and Byzantine techniques of yellow lead stannate and white tin oxide opacification of glasses to produce, first, yellow and, later, white opaque glazes (Tite et al. 2015; Matin et al. 2018; Fiorentino 2021). The earliest examples are Coptic Glazed Wares painted with lead stannate yellow glaze in discrete bands, found in several Umayyad-period sites (see Section 3.1.1). This technique was later developed to cover the overall surface of ceramics by lead-tin-oxide yellow or tin oxide white glazes, in the so-called Yellow Glazed Family wares of Syria and Palestine. From around the ninth century CE, lead-tin oxide yellow and tin oxide white glazes were used in the Samarra-type wares of Abbasid Mesopotamia. The opaque white glazed wares of Samarra-type pottery thrived as one of the most important and widely exported ceramics of the Islamic World (see Section 3). Subsequently, tin oxide white glazes spread throughout the Islamic world and became the mainstream opaque glazing technique used on medieval Islamic pottery.

The technology of tin-based opacification is based on one key ingredient: lead-tin calx. Lead-tin calx is the fine powder that is left after a mixture of lead and tin metals has been calcined (oxidised) by heating in air to their melting point and beyond to temperatures above 600°C, while occasionally stirring the mixture. The resulting calx powder varies in colour from whitish yellow, when lead content is negligible, to deep yellow, when it contains lead in considerable amounts. The calcination reaction, as outlined below, is controlled by the composition of the mixture.

$$Pb + O_2 \rightarrow 2PbO \tag{1}$$

$$Sn + O_2 \rightarrow SnO_2 \tag{2}$$

$$SnO_2 + 2PbO \rightarrow Pb_2SnO_4 \tag{3}$$

For tin oxide white glazes, the Pb/Sn ratio was kept less than the stoichiometric requirement of 3.5 for the formation of Pb_2SnO_4 in the reaction (3). Hence only the calcining reactions (1) and (2) occurred and the resulting calx would have contained a mixture of PbO and SnO_2, in addition to some unreacted SnO, Pb, and Sn. This type of lead-tin calx could have been used as a white colorant and opacifier in archaeological glass and glazes. The calx could have been mixed with either silica by itself, a mixture of silica and alkalis, or a pre-prepared glassy frit, and subsequently refired to produce a glass or glaze opacified by SnO_2 particles.

For opaque yellow glazes, the Pb/Sn ratio needed to be sufficient or more than the stoichiometric requirement of 3.5, so that the reactions (1), (2), and (3) were completed. The resulting calx powder therefore contained a combination of PbO, SnO_2, and Pb_2SnO_4, in addition to some unreacted SnO, Pb, and Sn. Previous XRD analysis of replicated lead-tin calces with Pb/Sn ratios of 7 and 30 fired to 600°C and 800°C confirmed that the calx mixture contained lead-tin oxide type I (Pb_2SnO_4), cassiterite (SnO_2), massicot (PbO, orthorhombic structure), and litharge (PbO, tetragonal structure) (Matin et al. 2018). The subsequent treatment of the calx depended upon the concentrations of alkalis in the final glass or glaze product. On this basis, the calx which contained Pb_2SnO_4 would have been subsequently treated in two different ways, namely lead-tin anima and lead-tin alkali frit.

To produce lead-tin anima, the calx was mixed with silica (SiO_2) and heated to above approximately 800°C to directly produce lead-tin-oxide yellow colorant and opacifier. During firing, variable amounts of SiO_2 substituted for SnO_2 in Pb_2SnO_4 (type I) which caused a crystalline conversion to $Pb(Sn,Si)O_3$ (type II) structures (Rooksby 1964; Kühn 1968; Clark et al. 1995; Matin et al. 2018). For this procedure to happen, the amounts of alkalis present must have been kept negligible (i.e., less than about 2 wt%). In the presence of alkali salts, a different set of reactions occur. Again, previous experiments demonstrated that during firing of a mixture of a calx, which contained Pb_2SnO_4 with silica and alkalis, $Pb(Sn,Si)O_3$ crystals decomposed and secondary SnO_2 crystals precipitated from the melt, and as a result, the colour of the glass or glaze changed from yellow to white (Matin et al. 2018). In order to prevent this dissolution from happening in alkali-rich compositions, the Pb_2SnO_4-containing calx was first mixed and heated with silica. The anima was then mixed with either pre-prepared alkali glass or alternatively with silica and alkalis and subsequently fired to produce primarily yellow glazes on ceramic tiles.

Producing lead-tin alkali frit required direct mixing of Pb_2SnO_4 containing calx (Pb/Sn > 3.5) with silica and alkalis and firing the mixture to temperatures above approximately 750°C which, depending upon the exact composition of the mixture, resulted in the dissolution of the lead-tin oxide and consequent precipitation of tin oxide particles and as a result, a white opaque alkali frit would form. The main application of this method was in opaque white pottery glazes as early as the eighth century in the Eastern Mediterranean (see Section 3.1.2), which continued as a primary glazing method in the Middle East, Central Asia, and Europe until the nineteenth century.

2.2 Lustre Decoration

Lustre is a thin (100 nm to 1 μm) decorative layer made of silver and/or copper nanoparticles that lies just beneath the surface of glass or glazed ceramic objects and provides them with metallic and iridescent appearance. The production of lustre was one of the most sophisticated technologies and required rigorous control of various factors. The lustre paint was a mixture of salts of silver and/or copper and a sulphur-containing compound, usually combined with an organic medium or clay to provide adhesion and workability. After the paint was applied on the surface of a finished glazed ceramic, the vessel was fired for the second time in a reducing atmosphere at approximately 500–600°C to avoid softening of the underlying glaze. Subsequent to this second firing, residues of unreacted lustre pigment were rubbed away from the glaze surface, revealing the lustre layer.

The reaction processes that took place during firing were crucial for the successful formation of lustre and involved two main stages. During the first stage, an ionic exchange between copper (Cu^+ or Cu^{2+}) and/or silver (Ag^+) cations in the lustre paint and the alkalis (Na_2O and K_2O) in the underlying glaze took place which resulted in the diffusion of copper/silver ions into the glaze.

During the second stage, the copper and silver cations in the glaze surface were reduced to metallic forms (i.e., Cu or Ag) to produce a thin layer of metallic nanoparticles (usually between 5 and 50 nanometres in diameter). The role of sulphur-containing compounds is critical in both these stages. In the first stage of the ionic exchange, the reaction of sulphur with copper and silver salts leads to enhanced diffusivity of copper and silver cations into the glaze. Sulphur also produces a locally reducing atmosphere which is necessary for the reduction of silver and copper cations to metallic forms in the second stage and the subsequent production of lustre layer. The composition of the underlying glaze also affected the final appearance of the lustre. As noted, the inclusion of alkalis in the glaze was vital for a successful ionic exchange with the lustre layer. Replication experiments by Molera et al. (2007) also demonstrated that the presence of lead in the glaze enhanced the metallic shine of the lustre decoration and resulted in the formation of a more highly concentrated nanoparticles layer (Pradell 2016: 14–15).

The colour and iridescent appearance of the final lustre can be variable and related to the optical response of the metal nanoparticles which often depends on their shape, size and concentration (Pradell 2016: 19–35). Pradell et al. (2008) showed that in general the Cu/Ag ratio in the original recipe determines the colour: yellow and green lustre tones were produced by silver-dominated paints, and amber, brown, and red by copper-dominated paints. If copper and silver ions dissolved or formed crystalline compounds in the glaze, different shades of yellow to green were produced.

Historical recipes for lustre provide unique insights into the ingredients and the processes of preparation that may not be otherwise understood given that the composition of the final lustre is different from that of the initial recipe. Jabir Ibn Hayyan's treatise (c. 721–815 CE) provides recipes for lustre on glass (Al-Hassan 2009). Recipes for lustre on glazed ceramics are given in the fourth chapter of *Jawāhir-Nāmeh-yi Nizāmī* by Jowhari Nishaburi, dated 1196 CE, and in the final chapter of *Arāyis al-Jawāhir va Nafāyis al-Atāyib* by Abu'l Qasim Kashani, dated 1301 CE (Matin 2020). The main ingredients were added either in the form of metallic copper/silver, burnt or roasted silver/copper (with impurities of metallic oxides), or silver/copper burnt with sulphur (Ag_2S and CuS). Sulphur was introduced either as a primary ingredient or from the decomposition of sulphur-containing compounds such as vitriol, alum ($K_2SO_4.$ $Al_2(SO_4)_3.24\ H_2O$), cinnabar (HgS), realgar (AsS), marcasite (FeS_2), or arseno-pyrite (FeAsS). Other metallic oxides, such as hematite (Fe_2O_3) or pyrolusite (MnO_2), were also added perhaps to act as reducing agents for silver/copper cations but also to act as colorant in the glaze; for instance, iron oxide produced pale green to yellow/brown and black, and manganese oxide produced purple to weak yellow/brown. The ingredients were ground (and sieved), mixed with vinegar or grape juice, and painted on vessels which were then fired in a specially designed kiln that was used to generate smoke and maintain a reducing atmosphere (Matin 2020: 484–485).

The earliest lustrewares emerged as part of the large corpus of Samarra-type pottery dated to ninth century CE (Section 4). From the late tenth century CE, and following the decline of the Abbasids, the production of lustrewares spread to Fatimid Egypt and subsequently to Northern Syria and Iran (Sections 4 and 5). The earliest Egyptian lustrewares appear on clay-based bodies but much of their development appear later on stonepaste bodies in Egypt, Syria, and Iran.

2.3 Stonepaste Bodies

Stonepaste ceramics (also referred to as quartz-frit, fritware, and faience), which consist of a crushed quartz body bonded together by a glassy phase, were likely first produced in Egypt during the eleventh century CE (Mason and Tite 1994), and were subsequently extensively produced throughout the Islamic Near East, particularly for finewares (Henderson 1989; Tite et al. 2011).

Abu'l-Qasim's treatise on the production of tiles and other ceramic objects in Iran, dating to about 1300 CE, describes stonepaste bodies as being made from some ten parts crushed quartz, one part crushed glass and one part fine white clay (Allan 1973). In the production of ceramics from this mixture, the clay provided the plasticity necessary for forming the quartz-rich body, and then, during firing, reacted with the glass fragments and, to a varying extent, with the crushed quartz to produce an extensive network of interparticle glass that bonded together the quartz body. The result was a hard, white body.

Table 1 provides a summary of representative compositions of selected Islamic stonepaste bodies from their beginnings in the eleventh century CE up until sixteenth century CE. Typically, the quartz contents are in the range 82–93 wt% SiO_2; the alumina contents, which provide a measure of the added clay, are in the range 2–6 wt% Al_2O_3; and the alkali contents, which provide a measure of the added glass, are in the range 2–5 wt% $Na_2O + K_2O$. In addition, in the case of Iznik ware, 1 wt% PbO contributes to the added glass. The principal exceptions to these concentration ranges are the ceramics from

Moshkin Tepe and the Jahan-Nama site in Isfahan, Iran, which contain lower quartz contents with higher alumina and alkali contents; and the so called 'proto- stonepaste' ceramic from Fustat (Fu P24).

The higher alumina contents of the stonepaste bodies from Moshkin Tepe and Jahan-Nama are likely due to the use of a high-alumina kaolinitic clay (Matin 2022; Aarab et al. 2025) which has the advantages of having high plasticity and being white firing. However, such clays are refractory and therefore, require a higher firing temperature. This explains the observed higher alkali contents of the Moshkin Tepe and Jahan-Nama stonepaste bodies compared to the other stone-paste bodies included in Table 2. Furthermore, the alkali-to-clay ratios (i.e., $(Na_2O + K_2O)/Al_2O_3$) tend to be higher in Moshkin Tepe Group II ceramics which exhibit more extensive vitrification.

In their 1994 paper on the beginnings of Islamic stonepaste ceramic production, Mason and Tite suggested that an important step in its evolution, after the move of potters from Abbasid Iraq to Fatimid Egypt during the later tenth century CE, was the production of, what they termed, 'a proto-stonepaste ceramic' which consisted of some five parts clay to which two parts crushed quartz and three parts glass were added. Subsequently, the amount of added crushed quartz was significantly increased whilst the amounts of clay and glass were reduced to achieve the relative proportions of the three components described in Abu'l-Qasim's treatise.

However, this evolution of the stonepaste technology proposed by Mason and Tite (1994) has recently been questioned by Matin and Ownby (2023). Based on a technological investigation of a group of eleven lustre and incised ware sherds from the rubbish grounds of Fustat (i.e., Old Cairo) in Egypt, which had previously been selected and studied art historically by Watson (1999a), they argued that an alternative explanation for the evolution of stonepaste production was achieved by the addition, in Egypt, of large amounts of crushed quartz to what had previously been clay bodies. Group I, the earliest samples, either did not include any glass fragments or contained only a few fragments (Figure 6a). As the technology developed, the amount of glass fragments added was increased significantly, and the result was the expected and required highly vitrified, compact, and white bodies, that is, Group II ceramics (Figures 6b and c).

Although siliceous bodies were used in the production of glazed ceramics in Iran in the Achaemenid (*c.*539–330 BCE) (Tite and Shortland 2004), it seems most unlikely that any knowledge of this technology survived into the Islamic period. However, wasters of Egyptian faience, which was produced using quartz-based bodies from the late fifth millennium BCE onwards (Matin and Matin 2012), have been found in a medieval Islamic context in Fustat and Iran.

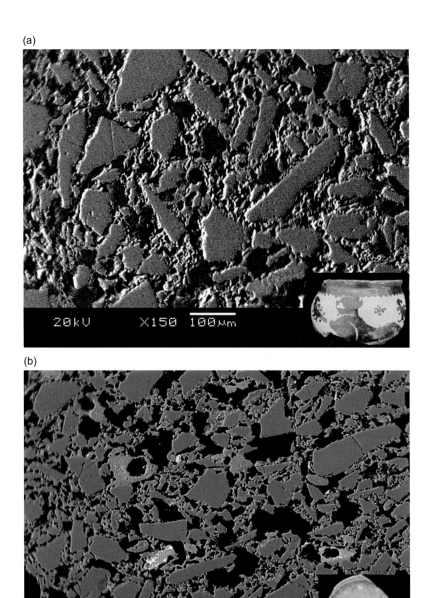

Figure 6 Backscattered SEM photomicrograph of stonepaste bodies of sherds from Fustat. (a) a lustre-painted sherd with the stonepaste Group I type body showing a stonepaste body made of fine-grained quartz with limited vitrification and no glass fragments (Victoria and Albert Museum, acc. no. C.772–1923), (b) a Fustat Fatimid Sgraffito (FFS) sherd with the stonepaste Group II body showing a stonepaste body made of fine-grained quartz with some glass fragments (Victoria and Albert Museum, sherd C.1054–1921), (Victoria and Albert Museum, acc. no. C.1615–1921).

(c)

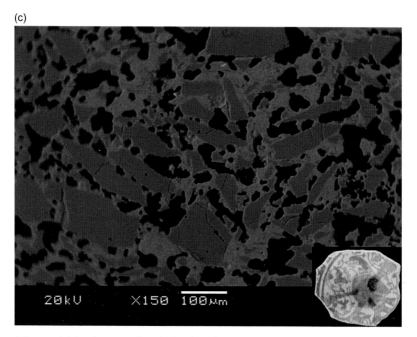

Figure 6 (c) a lustre-painted sherd with the stonepaste Group II type body showing extensive vitrification

This suggests that the production of faience was still continuing when the stonepaste technology emerged. The possibility for the Egyptian faience technology to have been the precursor to stonepaste ceramic bodies appears plausible, but at present, there is no direct evidence for this association.

It is generally argued that the introduction of stonepaste bodies was inspired, in part, by a desire of the Islamic potters to imitate imported Chinese porcelains without the necessity of access to an abundance of white firing clays and to a high temperature firing technology (Mason and Tite 1994). The fact that the monochrome incised wares produced in Fatimid Egypt in the eleventh century CE are clearly imitations of Song Dynasty *qingbai* porcelains supports this hypothesis. In addition, the predominance of stonepaste over clay bodies in the production of fineware ceramics from the Islamic Middle East probably also, in part, reflects the fact that quartz, as the major component of stonepaste bodies, was the same as far as the potter was concerned wherever it was found. Thus, when potters were moving from one area to another, quartz was a more 'predictable' material than the local clays whose properties would have had to have been carefully assessed before use if they were to form the bulk of the body. In contrast, when clay made up only some 10 wt% of the body, there would have been greater flexibility in what were acceptable properties.

Subsequent to the move of potters from Egypt towards the end of the eleventh century CE, the stonepaste technology reached Syria, Iran and beyond where it was used in the production of the great majority of Islamic fineware ceramics. A number of stonepaste workshops in India and Uzbekistan have survived to the present day. The last few remaining in Iran, in the cities of Shahreza, Meibod and Natanz, ceased production during the last ten years.

Compared to clay bodies, stonepaste bodies were more difficult to work. With the clay content usually around ten percent or less, they represented significantly less plasticity and workability, showcasing the potters' skills at their best working on pottery wheels or using moulds. Due to their reduced clay content, stonepaste bodies had fewer issues associated with clay bodies, such as water absorption or shrinkage. Being mainly composed of quartz, stonepaste bodies were particularly susceptible to thermal shocks during firing, such as the alpha-beta phase transition in quartz at about 570°C. Therefore, biscuit firing of stonepaste bodies could particularly increase the risk of pieces breaking in the kiln. Ethnographic reports from nineteenth-century stonepaste production in Iran by Centlivres-Demont (1971: 38–40), Wulff (1966: 166), and Bazl (1939: 1704–1705) all suggested that stone-pastes were raw-glazed, and thus far, no biscuit wasters have been found at any archaeological stonepaste production sites. However, without replication experiments, the full extent of different factors remains unclear.

2.4 Glazes

2.4.1 Glaze Types and Compositions

Table 2 provides a summary of representative compositions of transparent and opacified Islamic glazes from the eighth to sixteenth centuries CE. The high lead glazes (60–67 wt% PbO, < 2 wt% $Na_2O + K_2O$) were used for all the yellow glazes opacified with lead stannate, as well as for some white glazes opacified with tin oxide and some transparent glazes. Lead-alkali glazes (15–45 wt% PbO, 4–14 wt% $Na_2O + K_2O$) were used extensively for the white glazes opacified with tin oxide, as well for the transparent glazes. A small number of lead-alkali glazes with the lowest lead oxide contents are, perhaps, better termed alkali-lead glazes (4–5 wt% PbO, 10–12 wt% $Na_2O + K_2O$). Finally, soda-lime glazes (10–22 wt% Na_2O, 5–12 wt% CaO+MgO) were also extensively used for the transparent glazes.

Following on from Roman and Byzantine potters (Armstrong et al. 1997; Walton and Tite 2010), Islamic potters again produced the transparent high lead glazes either by applying lead oxide (or some other lead compound) by itself to the surface of the pottery body, or by applying a mixture of lead oxide-plus-quartz. With both methods, a small amount of clay can be included in the glaze slurry, and the application can be to either unfired or biscuit fired bodies. A further variation is that the lead oxide-plus-quartz mixture can be applied either in the raw state or after pre-fritting. As shown by Hurst and Freestone (1996), the two primary glazing methods can be distinguished by subtracting the percentages of lead oxide and any intentionally added colorant (e.g., copper oxide) from the glaze composition, and renormalising the resulting composition to 100%, as shown in the following equation:

$$C_i^* = \frac{C_i x\ 100}{\Sigma_{i+1}{}^N C_i - (C_{PbO} + C_{CuO})} \tag{2.4}$$

where C_i is the concentration of oxide i in the glaze and C_i^* is the adjusted concentration of oxide i. This adjusted glaze composition is then compared with the composition of the body. When glazing was by the application of lead oxide by itself, the adjusted glaze and the body compositions should be the same. In contrast, when glazing was by the application of a lead oxide-plus-quartz mixture, the silica content of the adjusted glaze should be higher than that of the body, and the alumina and other oxide contents should be lower.

Similarly, following on from the Seleucid (*c.*310–250 BCE), Parthian (*c.*250 BCE–226 CE) and Sassanian (226–637 CE) ceramics produced in Mesopotamia (McCarthy 1996), Islamic potters used soda-lime glazes produced from a soda-rich plant ash. However, soda-lime glazes appear to have been used much less frequently than high lead glazes. Instead, Islamic potters made extensive use of a hybrid lead-alkali glaze containing a very wide ranges of both lead oxide and alkali contents. One reason for extensive use by Islamic potters of glazes with a significant lead content is that a lead-tin calx is a key ingredient in the production of opaque white and yellow glazes, opacified respectively with tin oxide and lead stannate, which represents an important innovation introduced by Islamic potters (Section 2.1). Also, as a result, there are no tin-opacified soda-lime Islamic glazes.

In addition, high lead glazes have a number of advantages as compared to soda-lime glazes (Tite et al. 1998). First, because of the solubility of the alkali in water, the preparation and application of alkali glazes are more difficult than in the case of lead glazes. Second, a key advantage of lead glazes is that they provide a broad melting range. This results in a larger temperature window for firing the glaze, which is particularly significant in traditional ceramic kilns where temperature variations of up to 100°C could occur across different areas of the kiln. Further, the broad melting range also enables a more gradual transition from solid to liquid state during firing which allows the glaze to fully react and mature, resulting in smoother surfaces and better glaze bonding. In addition, lead glazes allow for better matching of thermal expansion with that of the body again reducing the risk of glaze 'crazing' during cooling; and their lower surface tension, as compared to that of alkali glazes, results in better 'wetting' properties which reduces the risk of glaze 'crawling'. Finally, lead glazes exhibit greater optical brilliance which increases with increasing lead content.

One advantage of lead-alkali glazes is that, as compared to high lead glazes, they have a higher viscosity in the molten state, resulting in a reduced mobility of the colorant ions and therefore, less running and merging of the associated colours. In addition, one potential problem with all lead glazes is the risk of reduction of lead oxide to lead metal which results in blackening and blistering of the glaze, and this risk is reduced as the lead content of the glaze is reduced. A further possible influence on the choice between high lead and lead-alkali glazes is the relative availability and cost of lead and soda-rich plant ash, depending on prevailing political and economic circumstances.

2.4.2 Glaze Colorants

In the production of glazed ceramics from their beginnings in fourteenth century BCE in Mesopotamia (Paynter 2008), through the Seleucid (*c.*310-250 BCE), Parthian (*c.*250 BCE–226 CE) and Sassanian (226–637 CE) periods again in Mesopotamia (McCarthy et al. 1996), to the Roman and Byzantine periods (Armstrong et al. 1997; Walton and Tite 2010), only a copper blue-green colorant was used until the emergence of Islamic glazed ceramics in the eighth century CE. By adapting the techniques employed by Byzantine glass workers, Islamic potters progressively extended their range of glaze colorants, both through the use of additional colorant ions dissolved in the glaze, and by the introduction of particulate colorants.

The principal ion-based colorants used by Islamic potters were copper (Cu^{2+}) for a range of blue-green colours, cobalt (Co^{2+}) for an intense blue colour, and manganese (Mn^{3+}) for a purple colour. In some cases, with the cobalt and manganese colorants, either the original mineral phases used as colorant are not entirely dissolved or new mineral phases precipitate. As a result, the colorant can have a particulate component as well providing ions in solution in the glaze.

The colour associated with copper ions depends first on the composition of the glaze in which it is dissolved. Thus, according to Weyl (1951: 163–167), copper ions produce a blue colour in an alkali-lime glaze, a turquoise colour in lead-alkali glaze, and a green colour in a high lead glaze. According to Ligand theory, these changes are the result of the stretching of electron orbitals which results in a change of wavelength. In addition, the nature of green colour of the glaze changes when other colorant ions, such as cobalt, iron, and chromium, are dissolved in the same area as the copper ions.

The particulate colorants first used by Islamic potters were their newly introduced opacifiers (Section 3.1), lead stannate yellow and tin oxide white. In addition, lead antimonate reappears as a yellow opaque colorant in Egypt in tenth century (Section 4.1.1) from where it spread to Tunisia and Sicily (Section 5.1.2).

The two other particulate colorants used by Islamic potters are bole red, which consists of a glassy frit containing a very fine mixture of quartz and haematite particles, and chromite black. Bole red appears to have been occasionally used as a colorant in the production of Raqqa underglaze decorated ware in the thirteenth century CE (Section 4.3.3). However, bole red was extensively used in the decoration of the later Iznik 'Rhodos' ware from about 1560 CE onwards.

Chromite black is an oxide mineral of the spinel group which can be represented by a chemical formula of the type $FeCr_2O_4$, where varying amounts of magnesium can substitute for the iron, ultimately forming $MgCr_2O_4$; and varying amounts of aluminium can substitute for the chromium, ultimately becoming $FeAl_2O_4$ (i.e., hercynite). In addition, as first observed in Iznik ware glazes (Tite 1989), chromite particles sometimes contain relatively significant amounts of copper, manganese, cobalt and nickel, which have diffused from the adjacent decorative colorants. Crushed, angular particles of chromite, which do not dissolve and diffuse within the glaze, were used to produce fine, black to dark-green linear underglaze decoration. As a refractory pigment, chromite was used to draw black to dark-green lines which prevented other coloured glazes from blending into each other.

Chromite was used as a pigment through much of the Islamic world. Its early application appears to be associated with slip-painted wares of Eastern Iran (Section 5.1.1), later extending to underglaze decorated (Section 5.2) and *mina'i* (Section 5.2.2) wares of Iran, as well as being used for Raqqa-type underglaze decorated wares of Syria (Section 4.3.3). Subsequently, its use is noted in Anatolia, first, by Seljuq potters (Section 6.1) and later, by Ottoman potters in the decoration of Miletus ware (Section 6.4) and Iznik ware (Section 6.5).

Two other decorative techniques used by Islamic potters were lustre decoration, as discussed in Section 2.2, and sgraffito decoration produced in Egypt (Section 4.1.2) in which incisions or carvings are made through an applied slip to reveal the contrasting colour of the underlying body.

In addition, the technique of *cuerda seca*, in which chromite was used to draw black to dark-green lines in order to prevent adjacent coloured glazes from blending into each other, began to be used in Iran in the Timurid period from the mid fourteenth century CE onwards, principally in the production of tiles rather than ceramic vessels (O'Kane 2011). However, being towards the end of the period, during which the majority of the ceramics considered in this paper date, the *cuerda seca* technique is not discussed further.

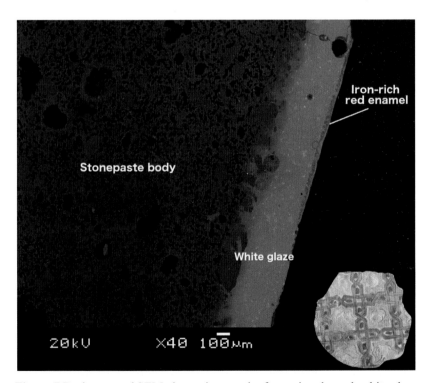

Figure 7 Backscattered SEM photomicrograph of a section through white glaze into the stonepaste body of a Persian *mina'i* sherd. The opaque white glaze is opacified by tin oxide particles, with a layer of iron-rich red enamel applied on top of the white glaze. The enamel shows as the darker part on the surface of the glaze. The stonepaste body appears to be highly vitrified (Victoria and Albert Museum, acc. no. 625.1868(6)).

2.4.3 Inglaze, Overglaze, and Underglaze Methods of Decoration

The three methods used to decorate glazed ceramics are *inglaze, overglaze* (or *onglaze*), and *underglaze* decoration. The *inglaze* technique involves applying decoration onto the surface of an unfired glaze, and allowing it to mature simultaneously with the glaze during firing. Second, the *overglaze* technique entails adding decorations to pottery after it has been glazed and fired. Once the decoration is applied, the pottery undergoes a further firing. Lustreware stands as the earliest example of *overglaze* decoration in the Islamic world. Another type of Islamic *overglaze* decorated pottery is represented by the Persian enamelled *mina'i* wares (e.g., see Figure 7). Finally, the *underglaze* technique involves painting directly onto the ceramic body, which is subsequently covered by a transparent glaze and fired (e.g., see Figure 8). This technique represents the final significant technological innovation in medieval Islamic pottery, and was initially extensively practiced in Iran, Egypt, and Syria in the twelfth and thirteenth centuries CE, later spreading to Anatolia and China.

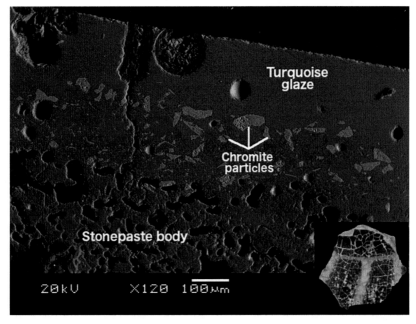

Figure 8 Backscattered SEM photomicrograph of a section through transparent turquoise glaze into the stonepaste body of an underglaze painted sherd from Moshkin Tepe, although it does not appear to be a local production. The black chromite pigment is applied on the surface of the stonepaste body and covered with a transparent turquoise glaze.

3 Eastern Mediterranean and Southern Mesopotamia

The establishment of the Islamic state in the seventh century brought about major political changes. These events, however, spurred little immediate cultural impact that can be identified in the ceramics of the first Islamic decades. The styles and technologies of seventh-century ceramics show little difference from those current immediately in the pre-Islamic period. Archaeological ceramic assemblages are dominated by utilitarian wares, including containers, cooking pots, serving wares (i.e., bowls, plates, and cups), lamps and lanterns, as well as tiles. Glazed wares represent only a small minority. In southern Mesopotamia, the production of Parthian and Sasanian monochrome green- and turquoise-glazed jars continued into the Islamic period, but again little changes took place in this early period.

It was towards the late eighth century that radical changes took place. As Walmsley (2007: 54) put it, this transformation process is 'recognisable as a cultural "punctuation point" due to the decisiveness of the stylistic changes involved'. The material culture evidence often discussed in keeping with this cultural punctuation point is the coinage reform of the Umayyad period. Ceramics, despite the versatility and cruciality of evidence they provide, have largely been neglected. Most notable among the drastic changes that took place in the Eastern Mediterranean in the eighth century were the development of regional fine wares, as well as the emergence of Islamic glazed wares.

3.1 Eastern Mediterranean

During the Roman period, the development and market demand economy for fine tableware pottery was well established across the Eastern Mediterranean (see e.g., Brughmans and Poblome 2016). The most common types, such as fine red-slipped terra sigillata wares of North Africa and Cyprus, had glossy, smooth surfaces despite lacking glaze. The termination of this trade encouraged further regional productions of unglazed fine pottery in the Eastern Mediterranean. By the late eighth century, Jarash bowls, painted red terracotta wares, pale orange wares, as well as Fine Byzantine wares (also known as Palestinian Fine wares; see Walmsley 2007: 53) developed to replace Late Roman fine wares that had become increasingly unavailable (Walmsley 2007: 52–54; Rottenborg and Blanke 2017: 322–323). It was also in this context that Islamic glazed ceramics emerged and represented new technological inventions and styles. The earliest phase of Islamic glazed ceramics is represented by Coptic Glazed wares (CGW), Cream wares, and Hijazi wares, and their further developments into the Yellow Glaze Family (YGF) wares.

3.1.1 Coptic Glazed Wares, Cream Wares, and Hijazi Wares

The term Coptic Glazed Ware (CGW) was first used by Rodziewicz (1976: 63–64) to designate an assemblage of bowls excavated in Kom el-Dikka, Alexandria, Egypt, that occurred immediately after late Roman levels. Further excavations have identified CGW in various sites across Egypt, Jordan, Palestine, and Syria (for a review see Matin et al. 2018: 43). Petrographic studies have shown that the light orange-coloured bodies of CGW were made of kaolinitic clay from the Aswan region, Egypt (Matin et al. 2018; Salinas et al. 2019; Ting and Taxel 2020), which confirms earlier propositions of Egyptian manufacture by Rodziewicz (1976, 1978, 1983) and Whitcomb (1989) based on stylistic forms. CGW are characterised by open dish forms with flat bases, copying styles of Late Roman fine wares (Figure 9a). The bodies are covered with a thin white/greyish slip (Figure 9b; see also, Ting and Taxel 2020) and either painted and covered with an overall high-lead translucent amber glaze, or decorated in discrete bands with high-lead opaque yellow, green, and/or brown glazes, with some areas left unglazed. The latter type of CGW, decorated with bands of opaque glazes, are significant in that they represent the first examples of the invention and use of tin-based opacification technology of ceramic glazes. Chemical analyses by Ting and Taxel (2020: Table 4) and Matin et al. (2018: Table 7) have shown 55–75 wt% PbO and up to 2.5 wt% SnO_2 and negligible alkalis (< 0.3 wt% $Na_2O + K_2O$) in the opaque glazes. The glazes were opacified by the use of lead stannate type II ($Pb(Sn,Si)O_3$) in the glaze with the Pb/Sn ratios usually

(a)   (b)

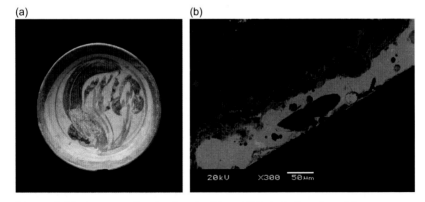

Figure 9 (a) An example of a Coptic Glazed Ware (Ashmolean Museum, acc. no. EA1974.48); (b) a typical backscattered SEM photomicrograph of a section through opaque yellow glaze into the slip and body of a Coptic Glazed Ware.

greater than 35, representing the calx composition (for the opacification technology see Section 2.1). In the yellow glazes, the lead stannate also acted as the yellow colorant, but in the green and brown glazes, copper oxide and manganese oxide were added respectively as the colorants. For the translucent amber glazes, iron oxide was used as the colorant. The subsequent developments of tin-based opacification of glazes are seen in the so-called Yellow Glazed Family wares (Section 3.1.2) and later in Samarra-type wares (Section 3.2.2).

Cream wares (also known as Mefjar ware after their discovery at Khirbat Mafjar near Jericho) were found at various archaeological sites in Syria, Palestine, and Jordan dated to the late eighth to ninth century and were suggested to have been produced in the Syria-Palestine region (see Walmsley 2001). They are characterised by pale cream bodies, often in the form of delicate, thin-walled jars, jugs, and water flasks with incised, appliqué, and moulded decoration. A variety labelled 'Cream Splash ware' is suggested by Whitcomb (1991: 53) to have been a close descendant of CGW. Cream Splash wares are similar to CGW both in their open dish forms as well as in the styles of paintings applied under high-lead transparent glazes. Another derivative of CGW were the Hijazi ware, after excavation of assemblages and wasters of glazed wares throughout the Hijaz (Hamed 1988). Hijazi wares exhibit similar painting motifs to CGW, although also often show cross-hatching decoration applied on dark red-orange fabric which Whitcomb (1991: 53) proposed may suggest later developments. Comprehensive compositional and mineralogical analysis of the bodies and glazes of Cream wares and Hijazi wares are still largely lacking which hinders further interpretations on provenance and use of raw materials.

3.1.2 Yellow Glazed Family

Further development and use of CGW decorative techniques is characterised in ceramics excavated throughout Syria and Anatolia, including for instance at Tell Aswad/Raqqa (Watson 1999b), Al-Mina (Vorderstrasse 2005: 75–78), Qinnasrin (Whitcomb 1999: 81–83), Antioch (Waagé 1948), and Tarsus (Bagci 2016). The wares were labelled 'Yellow Glaze Family' (YGF) by Watson (1999b: 81) after his classification of the sherds from Tell Aswad/Raqqa, and are characterised by their broad-based bowl shapes and the reddish to pale yellow colour of their bodies (see Figure 4). Despite its name, the YGF encompasses not only opaque yellow glazed wares but the first examples of opaque white glazed wares, with green and/or brown decorations. Of all the ceramics found in the above archaeological sites, YGF wares make up one of the main types in the corpus; three-quarters of the excavated glazed sherds in Tell Aswad, for instance (Watson 1999b).

YGF wares were made from calcareous clays containing 10–20 wt% CaO. The yellow glazes are of the very high lead type containing greater than 60 wt% PbO and negligible alkali (<2 wt% $Na_2O + K_2O$) and the white glazes of the high lead-alkali type containing 35–50 wt% PbO and 3–6 wt% $Na_2O + K_2O$ (Matin et al. 2018). The yellow glazes were opacified by lead stannate (Pb(Sn, Si)O_3) crystals with the Pb/Sn ratios greater than 16, representing the calx composition, and the white glazes by tin oxide crystals with the Pb/Sn ratios varying between 2.5 and 9 (see Section 2.1). In the green and brown glazes, copper oxide and manganese oxide were used as colorants.

3.2 Southern Mesopotamia

The developments seen in the early Islamic period in Southern Mesopotamia, that is, the region of southern Iraq and western Iran, appear to have been both a continuation and development of earlier pre-Islamic traditions in the region as well as the innovations that took place during the eighth century in the Eastern Mediterranean. While the production of monochrome green and turquoise-glazed jars continued into the Islamic period, new ceramic types with radically novel range of decorations were produced in the ninth century, referred to as the 'Samarra-type' pottery after the city they were first excavated. The corpus brought about a transformation in the study of the history of ceramic manufacture and provided unique evidence of production and consumption of fine glazed pottery in the early Abbasid period as well as the dynamics and impact of trade with Tang China.

3.2.1 Monochrome Green- and Turquoise-Glazed Jars

Being one of the most long-lasting pottery traditions, the manufacture of monochrome green- and turquoise-glazed jars in southern Mesopotamia during the Parthian and Sasanian periods continued into the Umayyad and early Abbasid periods. Over the twelve centuries of their production (from third century BCE to tenth century CE), the jars were made using calcareous alluvial clays from Mesopotamia and covered by alkali glazes (see, e.g., Hill 2006; Pace et al. 2008). The glazes were coloured by dissolved copper but the difference in green and turquoise colours are not currently fully understood. Further subdivisions based on the appearance of glazes, body fabrics, and forms in different assemblages have also been suggested by archaeologists (see, e.g., Priestman 2005: 234–240; Kennet 2004; Boucharlat 1993). The jars show a considerable variation in sizes, usually from about 20 to 80 cm height, and are decorated by different techniques including appliqué, thumb impressed ridges, and incision. After the eighth century, the range of designs (Priestman 2016: 2–3) and the scale of production expanded, and the jars became a significant object of trade.

The main purpose of these jars was the storage and transport of foodstuffs – especially date and date-syrup, but also oils and cane sugar (Wright 1984: 44). They were distributed widely for their contents throughout upper Mesopotamia, East Africa, the Persian Gulf, Southeast Asia, and the Far East (see, e.g., Priestman 2021). In China, archaeological remains of green glazed jars were found as early as the late Eastern Han period (25–220 CE) in a tomb in Hepu. In general, they were mostly associated with the ports of Yangzhou and Guangzhou, where Middle Eastern merchants and communities resided, or at Buddhist monasteries where the contents of the jars would have been valued for their medicinal or ritual purposes (Cheng 2016: 58–63 cited in Wen 2018: 324).

By the tenth century, the manufacture of monochrome green- and turquoise-glazed jars went through a decline. The political and social turmoil of the tenth century and the weakening of the Abbasid empire may have been partially responsible. Harvey (2021) argued, based on the study of early Islamic textual documents, that the prophet's hadith/saying in which the use of green-glazed jars for the storage or fermentation of date-wine was prohibited may have contributed to such decline. The invention of white tin-opacified glazing technology and the development of the so-called Samarra-type wares may also have been a contributing reason, although green-glazed jars still continued for about a century after the proliferation of Samarra wares.

3.2.2 Samarra-Type Pottery

The Abbasid palatial city of Samarra, Iraq, was founded in 836 CE and abandoned in 884 CE. The excavation of the site before the First World War and the subsequent publication of ceramics by Sarre (1925) marked a major turning point in the understanding of Islamic ceramics. The so-called 'Samarra-type' or 'Samarra-horizon' pottery, dated to the middle of ninth century, was characterised by exceptionally fine open bowl shapes, covered by opaque white glaze with a range of inglaze or overglaze decorations (see Northedge and Kennet 1994: 23–25; Whitehouse 1979). In addition, the Samarra excavations unearthed an unprecedented number of imported Chinese stonewares of the Tang dynasty. The most typical shapes of Samarra-type wares, typically with shallow curved profiles and a rounded flared rim, were almost exact copies of Chinese wares. The vessels were entirely covered by a background opaque white glaze, imitating the smooth, white surfaces of imported Chinese wares. The white surfaces were then either left plain, or decorated with a range of new innovative techniques executed by local potters, including blue (and green)-on-white, green-splashed, or lustre overglaze decorations (Northedge and Kennet 1994).

The bodies of Samarra-type wares are made of buff-coloured fine-grained Southern Mesopotamian calcareous clays (20–25 wt% CaO), hitherto widely designated as 'Basra fabric' (see, e.g., Mason 2004; Hallett 2000). It appears, however, that the alluvial geology of the region is very homogenous for the purpose of petrofabric studies, and therefore similar clay types could have been used in various production centres over this vast geographic region. The petrographic fabrics and compositions of the bodies do not appear sufficiently distinctive to make secure suggestions concerning provenance (Matin et al. 2018: 47; see also, Priestman 2011). In order to avoid any misinterpretation, the term 'Southern Mesopotamian fabric' is preferred here which refers to the alluvial plains of southern Iraq and Iran, rather than a specific site of production.

White glazes of Samarra-type pottery are of three compositional types and represent different compositions and microstructures: (1) Alkali glazes containing 12–15 wt% $Na_2O + K_2O$ and less than 1 wt% PbO. These glazes show a combination of air bubbles, partially reacted quartz and other mineral particles dispersed throughout the thickness but are not opacified by tin oxide particles. This glaze type was widely practiced in southern Mesopotamia during the pre-Islamic period (see, e.g., Paynter 2001). (2) Alkali-lead glazes containing 10–12 wt% $Na_2O + K_2O$ and 5–15 wt% PbO. The glazes are opacified by tin oxide particles, with Pb/Sn ratios of approximately 1 (see Section 2.1), as well as containing air bubbles and quartz grains. (3) High lead-alkali type containing 35–50 wt% PbO and 3–6 wt% $Na_2O + K_2O$. The glazes are again opacified by tin oxide with calx Pb/Sn ratios between 2.5 and 9.

Blue-on-White Wares

The blue-on-white and blue plus green-on-white are generally considered to be the earliest wares of the Samarra-type pottery. The glazes are of the alkali-lead and non-tin opacified alkali compositional types. The cobalt pigment was painted in geometric, palmette, or epigraphic patterns into the dry surface of raw glaze and then fired in the kiln. Compositional analyses of the cobalt blue glaze show that the pigment was of the Fe-Co-Zn type. The workshops that produced these wares are not known, but the various methods of painting and ways of pigment preparation (Wood et al. 2009), as well as their decorative patterns have been tentatively suggested to be related to different workshops (Tamari 1995: 127–145).

It appears that Samarra-type blue-on-white wares had exerted an influence on the production of the first high fired wares with blue decoration in China. The evidence comes from the Belitung shipwreck, a dhow from the Persian Gulf that sank near the Belitung Island, Indonesia, on its way to the Middle East around the second quarter of the ninth century (Guy 2005; Smithsonian Institute 2011). The cargo contained three pieces of Chinese blue-and-white Tang stonewares painted in cobalt blue. The designs with palmettes were clearly Islamic, directly similar to those seen on Samarra-type blue-on-white wares. Most probably produced at the Gongxian kilns for the Middle Eastern market, these three dishes represent China's first high fired wares with cobalt blue decoration (Krahl 2001). The most important development of Chinese blue-and-white porcelain however took place about five centuries later during the Mongol Yuan period, and there is no evidence to support direct technological or stylistic continuation.

Green-Splashed Wares

The green-splashed wares are associated with all three glaze compositional types. The green glazes were coloured by dissolved copper and show elevated zinc contents (see, e.g., Matin et al. 2018). The origins of the splashed designs have been a subject of controversy. While it has been argued that these were imitation of imported Chinese Sancai wares (see, e.g., Rawson et al. 1988), Watson (2014) suggested that the designs were an independent Islamic invention and related to early Islamic glazed wares of the Eastern Mediterranean, commonly used, for instance, on the Yellow Glazed Family wares (see Susa assemblage; see also Wen 2018, 297–298).

Lustreware

The lusterwares of Samarra-type pottery represent the first examples of the application of lustre decoration on ceramic glazes (see Figure 5). The intricate patterns are precisely executed and often cover the entire surface of the wares. There are three main groups of lustrewares in Samarra, that is polychrome lustre, ruby lustre, and monochrome golden lustre. Although the chronology of Abbasid lustrewares is still not certain, it is generally agreed that the polychrome and ruby lustrewares dated to the ninth century and monochrome lustre to the tenth century (Northedge and Kennet 1994). The polychrome lustre contained both copper and silver and showed three to five colours. Ruby lustres were rich in copper and monochrome lustres were rich in silver. The lustre decorations were applied over alkali-lime glazes opacified by a combination of air bubbles and unreacted mineral particles, or over tin-oxide opacified alkali-lead glazes. Pradell et al. (2008) argued that the transition from polychrome to monochrome lustres may have been coincident with that from alkali to alkali-lead glazes. The presence of lead in the underlying glaze facilitated the formation of silver metal particles which may have in turn led to the shift in the production from copper-and-silver-based polychrome lustres to silver-rich mono-chrome lustres. In some of the lustre and the blue (and green)-on-white decorated wares, grey glazes appear in place of white. It has been unclear whether their application was a deliberate effect or a result of misfiring or weathering during subsequent burial (see, e.g., Northedge and Kennet 1994: 33).

3.2.3 Susa Assemblage

Another key archaeological assemblage of Samarra-type pottery was found in Susa, Iran (Kervran 1977, 1979; Guillermina et al. 2005). The pottery assemblage includes all the typical wares discussed above (i.e., blue-on-white, green splashed, and lusterwares) as well as a wide range of opaque yellow and white glazed wares. The significance of these latter wares is in that they indicate striking similarities to the earlier Coptic Glazed Wares and Yellow Glazed Family wares of the Eastern Mediterranean, particularly in their shape, design, and glazing techniques. Essentially in the form of shallow bowls with flat bases or low footrings and steep walls, the wares were entirely covered by opaque yellow and white glazes decorated with geometrical designs or with runs of green and/or brown from the rim. The composition of opaque yellow glazes of these Samarra-type wares are similar to those of Coptic and Yellow Glazed Family wares of Eastern Mediterranean, containing very high lead oxide contents (> 60 wt% PbO) and opacified by the proliferation of lead-stannate crystals. The green and brown glazes were again achieved using respectively copper and manganese oxides which have blended into underlying tin-opacified white glaze (Matin et al. 2018).

The evidence from the Susa assemblage further reinforces the connections with the earlier ceramic inventions that had taken place in the Eastern Mediterranean. The eastwards transfer of technologies and styles from the Eastern Mediterranean to Mesopotamia may have been related to the movement of the Islamic capital from Damascus, Syria, to Baghdad, Iraq, after the over-throw of the Umayyads by the Abbasids in 762 CE, which may have encouraged the migration of craftspeople and technologies.

4 Egypt and Syria

'Al-Fustat of Misr in the present day is like Baghdad of Old. I know of no city in Islam superior to it'. Al-Muqadassi (quoted in Hourani 1995: 79) wrote in about 983/4 CE, some fifteen years after the conquest of the Fatimids in Egypt. The Fatimid period in Egypt (969–1171 CE) was one of abundant construction, agricultural and industrial productivity, and a well-established network of trade. Meanwhile, Iraq under the Abbasids was experiencing political and economic instability leading to the migration of people and knowledge to Egypt, which was rapidly becoming a thriving centre of commerce and innovation. This movement is evident in the ceramics of this period, as early Egyptian lustrewares showed monochrome lustre designs that were similar to those practiced in Abbasid Iraq. Given the intricate complexity of the lustre technique, it is challenging to envision means of knowledge exchange other than the movement of the potters and their skills. However, potters in Egypt used local Nile alluvium clay to produce ceramic bodies, rather than the southern Mesopotamian calcareous clay that was used on Samarra-type wares. It also appears that the white tin-opacified glazes have lead/tin ratios different than those of Samarra-type pottery which conveys the use of different calx recipes in Egypt.

The favourable economic conditions in Fatimid Egypt also encouraged new innovations in ceramic production. A variety of new glaze colorants were introduced, such as lead antimonate yellow for use in polychrome wares (Section 4.1.1), and the use of cobalt blue expanded beyond Iraq to Egypt. During the Fatimid Dynasty, the centre of maritime trade with the Far East shifted from the Persian Gulf to the Red Sea, leading to an influx of imported Chinese porcelains in Egypt. To provide more affordable alternatives to these imported Chinese porcelains, potters developed stonepaste bodies that resembled the whiteness and compactness of Chinese porcelain. This development of stonepaste appears to have been an Egyptian innovation, as there is evidence of experimental phase closely linked to the production of lustrewares and the so-called Fustat Fatimid Sgraffito wares.

It has been suggested that stonepaste ceramic technology was transmitted from Egypt to Syria and Iran. This hypothesis is supported by two main factors. Firstly, there has so far been no evidence of an experimental phase in either Syria or Iran, which suggests that the technology was likely introduced from outside these regions. Additionally, the Syrian Tell Minis lustrewares, which are the earliest known Syrian lustrewares, bear a striking resemblance to Egyptian lustrewares, further supporting the idea of transfer from Egypt. However, it should be noted that in Syria, the earliest stonepaste ceramics are represented by the incised and carved decorated wares, rather than lustrewares. According to

Tonghini (1998: 41), further evidence is necessary to determine whether the absence of lustre-decorated stonepaste in the earliest phases of archaeological sites in Syria may simply be due to their limited spread during the initial phase of production.

During the subsequent Ayyubid (1171–1250) and Mamluk (1250–1517) periods in Egypt and Syria, the production of stonepaste pottery continued, with widespread trade and distribution. New decorative styles, including under-glaze painting, emerged and despite the ongoing debate about their origins in Syria, Egypt, or Iran, they signify a significant technological advancement that endured for centuries and exerted influence on subsequent ceramic traditions in China (for a full discussion see Section 5).

4.1 Glazed Clay-Bodied Wares

Egyptian and Syrian pottery include a strong tradition of earthenwares with polychrome and incised decoration. While some appear to demonstrate a continuation and further evolution of Byzantine ceramic practices, others, such as lusterware, introduce entirely novel approaches to pottery production in these regions.

4.1.1 Polychrome Glazed Ceramic Production in Egypt

Following on from Coptic Glazed Ware (Section 3.1.1), polychrome glazed ceramics continued to be produced into the second half of the ninth century. These ceramics were previously occasionally referred to as the 'Fayyumi wares' after a substantial number of them were discovered in the Italian excavations in the Fayyum region, although no evidence of production or wasters have so far been found. Similar to the Coptic Glazed Wares, the polychrome glazed wares were made of pink bodies using the kaolinitic clay from Aswan and with comparable very high lead glazes (about 60 wt% PbO, $<$ 1 wt% $Na_2O + K_2O$) (Salinas et al. 2019). However, although these glazes contained some 1 wt% SnO_2, no particulate lead stannate or tin oxide were now detected (Salinas et al. 2019).

Next, through into the tenth century, polychrome opaque glazed ceramics, with calcareous clay bodies (16–25 wt% CaO) and high lead glazes (40–60 wt% PbO, 2–6 wt% $Na_2O + K_2O$), were produced in the Fustat region near to modern Cairo from the second half of 9th century through into 10th century (Salinas et al. 2019). These ceramics may include as many as six different glaze colours (yellow, amber, green, turquoise, white, and brown) which are applied side by side forming colour bands occupying the whole surface of the ceramic. However, instead of lead stannate, the yellow and amber glazes are coloured and opacified by particulate lead antimonate together with higher amounts of dissolved iron as compared to the other glaze colours. The antimony oxide contents are in the range 1.0–1.7 wt% Sb_2O_3 for the amber glazes and 0.2–0.5 wt% Sb_2O_3 for the yellow. The iron oxide contents vary from 2.4 to 2.8 wt% FeO for the amber glazes, and 1.3–2.3 wt% FeO for the yellow glazes. The green glazes are coloured by dissolved copper (0.9–1.3 wt% CuO) and opacified with lead antimonate (0.2–0.9 wt% Sb_2O_3). Turquoise glazes are again coloured by dissolved copper (0.2–2.6 wt% CuO) but opacified with tin oxide, and the brown are coloured by dissolved manganese (1.5–4.1 wt% MnO).

Next, with the Fatimid conquest of Egypt in 969 CE and the foundation of Fustat as the capital of the Fatimid dynasty, calcareous clay bodies, high lead glazes, and lead antimonate and tin oxide opacifiers continued to be used. Initially, the ceramics were decorated with transparent yellow and green glazes, coloured respectively with dissolved iron and copper oxides, over a white tin-opacified background. These ceramics were similar in appearance to the earlier polychrome ceramics produced in Tunisia except that, in Tunisia, a tin-opacified white glaze was not used for the white background, as discussed in Section 5.1.

Subsequently, in Egypt, the ceramics were decorated with areas of lead antimonate opacified yellow glaze, together with areas of transparent green glaze, which spread over a substantial area of the white tin-opacified background.

Rediscovery of Lead Antimonate Yellow

The fact that lead antimonate yellow was used in the production of Egyptian ceramics from the second half of ninth century CE suggests that the technology for the production of lead stannate yellow, which involved firing a fairly specific mixture of lead/tin calx and quartz at a temperature of about 850°C (Matin et al. 2018), had been lost in Egypt by that time. Its replacement, lead antimonate, had previously been used to produce opaque yellow glass in Egypt and the Near East from about 1500 BCE until the fourth century CE. Then, Roman glass producers switched to the use of lead stannate yellow, together with tin oxide white in place of calcium antimonate previously used for the production of opaque white glass.

The question therefore arises as to how Egyptian potters of the early Islamic period rediscovered the yellow lead antimonate opacifier in the second half of the ninth century CE. In view of the gap in time from the fourth to the second half of the ninth century, it seems very unlikely that the Islamic potters rediscovered lead antimonate as a result of surviving written documentation or an oral tradition of its past use. Instead, it is suggested by Salinas et al. (2019) that the Egyptian potters experimented with various available minerals, including the antimony mineral, stibnite (Sb_2S_3), and the lead mineral, galena (PbS), which frequently contains stibnite impurities, with a view to increasing their available palette of colours for the production of polychrome glazed ceramics. As a result, three opaque colours (yellow, amber, and green) emerged, all opacified with lead antimonate.

Lead antimonate pigments can be produced by heating mixtures of lead and antimony oxides together with a flux, such as sodium chloride, which increases the reactivity of the oxides and results in the $Pb_2Sb_2O_7$ structure rather than a mixture of lead antimony oxides. However, in the case of glazes, a flux is not necessary since as soon as the pigment in added to the glaze, it will react with the lead, dissolve in the glass and recrystallise as $Pb_2Sb_2O_7$.

The fact that the Islamic potters used lead antimonate yellow together with tin oxide white, in contrast to the Roman glassmakers who used calcium antimonate white, supports the argument that lead antimonate yellow was rediscovered in the second half of the ninth century by experimenting with stibnite/galena minerals, rather than through the recovery of the Roman technological tradition

4.1.2 Sgraffito

Sgraffito (or sgraffiato) wares are characterised by slip-painted earthenwares with incisions or carvings through the slip into the body, and covered with a transparent lead-based glaze. In Egypt, sgraffito wares appear to have developed from the local polychrome glazed wares (Bongianino 2014: 33), characterised by porous pink, red, or buff clay bodies which are typically composed of Nile alluvium clay or mixtures with calcareous clay. The ceramics bodies are covered with a quartz-based slip (Mason and Keall 1990), and subsequently glazed. A parallel-hatched incision is commonly seen on these wares.

Syrian sgraffito wares represent light orange to pink bodies depending on the amount of lime present. Based on analysis of a small number of samples by Mason 2004, the high lead glaze appears to contain 60–65 wt% PbO and is usually coloured amber/yellow by iron oxide or green by copper oxide. The glaze is sometimes splashed with copper-oxide green, iron-oxide amber/brown, and manganese-oxide purple/dark brown.

4.1.3 Lustrewares

The early phase of Egyptian lustreware production is represented by earthenwares with tin-opacified glazes and showed close stylistic links with the Abbasid monochrome lustrewares of the Samarra-type pottery (Philon 1980).

Based on the earliest pieces with datable inscriptions, it appears that production had begun by the year 1000 CE.

The earthenware body was typically composed of Nile alluvium clay mixed with calcareous clay (approx. 20 wt% CaO, 10 wt% Al_2O_3). Through experimentation, it appears that significant amounts of quartz were added to the otherwise clay body, resulting in a transition towards early stonepaste bodies that contained only around 30% clay (discussed in Section 2.3). The glazes were of the lead-alkali compositional type (25–35 wt% PbO, 5–9 wt% $Na_2O + K_2O$) and opacified by typically 2.5–12 wt% SnO_2 (Matin and Ownby 2023). Based on microprobe analysis of lustre layers in six samples, Pradell et al. (2008: 2652) showed that the lustre layers on some of the samples are silver-rich with minimal copper (2–2.9 wt% Ag, 0.2 wt% Cu) others are made of a combination of copper and silver (1 – 1.9 wt% Cu, 1.8–5.4 wt % Ag).

4.1.4 Turquoise-Glazed Wares

Found at various sites across the Euphrates from Syria down to Northern Iraq, including Qal'at Ja'bar, Qasr al-Hayr al-Sharqi, and 'Ana. Turquoise-glazed wares appear to have been produced between the twelfth and fourteenth centuries and were most probably introduced contemporaneously to the Syrian stonepaste Tell-Minis wares (see Section 4.3). The buff to pink coloured body was made of calcareous clay with mixed sand, which may have been naturally present or deliberately added as a temper. They are noticeably distinct in form from the pre-Islamic and early Islamic turquoise glazed jars of southern Mesopotamia, discussed in Section 3.2.1, and open-form tablewares are often discovered, although closed forms are also present.

4.2 Egyptian Stonepaste Wares

Egyptian glazed stonepaste pottery has been found in substantial numbers in Fustat, near modern Cairo. Excavations were directed by Bahgat between 1912 and 1920 and a report on pottery was published in 1930 (Bahgat and Massoul 1930). Systematic excavations by an American team directed by Scanlon in the late 1960s provided the first stratigraphic evidence, and this was followed by data from French excavations at Istabl 'Antar directed by Gayraud (see, e.g., Scanlon 1984; Gayraud 2017). However, the assessment of the archaeological record obtained from the excavations has been difficult due to various factors. These include the turbulent history of Fustat, marked by multiple phases of destruction and abandonment, as well as the insufficient documentations in preliminary archaeological reports. To date, a detailed chronology of Fustat stonepaste pottery is not fully understood and the dating is often based on stylistic comparison and the study of inscriptions (see Philon 1980). The chemical analysis of the bodies and glazes of Egyptian pottery reported here is often restricted to a limited number of sherds, and further research is undoubtedly necessary to understand the entire scope of their production.

The evolution of stonepaste bodies in Egypt was closely linked with the development of lustrewares and the so-called Fustat Fatimid Sgraffito (FFS) wares (see Figures 6a–c). The progressive development is seen in transition from bodies with fine sized quartz mixed with few frit fragments (but not always), to those composed of finer quartz, significantly more frit, and consequently exhibiting higher vitrification and a harder and more compact body (Matin and Ownby 2023). These represent one of the peaks of stonepaste pottery throughout its extensive and diverse history. The Persian traveller Nassir Khusraw who visited Egypt in 1047, described the pottery as 'so delicate that one can see his hand through it when held up in the light' (Nassir Khusraw 2001: 72), suggesting that they had achieved a level of quality with vitreous bodies that allowed for translucency (see Watson 2015). The development of stonepaste bodies appears to correspond with the development of glazing technology in Fustat from tin-opacified to transparent lead-alkali glazes. This could suggest that with the development of stonepaste bodies, there was no longer a need for white opaque glazes, thus leading to the transition to transparent glazes.

The discussion below has primarily focused on two main types of stonepaste wares: lustrewares and the Fustat Fatimid Sgraffito (FFS) wares. However, it is important to note that Egypt's involvement in pottery production extended beyond these mentioned types. For example, a significant quantity of sherds and a waster from polychrome glazed *laqabi* wares, typically associated with the Syrian Tell Minis wares (as discussed in Section 4.3.1), were discovered in Fustat. Furthermore, there have been recent findings identifying a number of *mina'i* enamel decorated wares, a technique originating from Iran (see Section 5.2.2), as Egyptian productions (Watson 2024). These discoveries affirm Egypt's active participation in the dynamic production of a diverse range of stonepaste pottery.

4.2.1 Lustrewares

The lustre-decorated stonepaste wares of Egypt represent striking designs, typically featuring central figural motifs either drawn in lustre on a plain background or in reverse on a lustre background. A wide range of lustre colours were used, most commonly yellow, green, and brown, derived from different copper and silver amounts (Pradell et al. 2008; see also Section 2). The stonepaste bodies are composed of around 85 wt% SiO_2, 4–4.5 wt% Al_2O_3 and 2.5–5 wt% CaO and as discussed above exhibit a range of petrofabrics with minimal to extensive vitrification (approximately 2–4 wt% $Na_2O + K_2O$). The glazes are of the lead-alkali compositional types containing 20–35 wt% PbO and 6–11 wt% $Na_2O + K_2O$ which were opacified with 5.5–19 wt% SnO_2, sometimes coloured green/turquoise by copper oxide, or blue by cobalt oxide (Mason 2004; Matin and Ownby 2023). The wide range of tin oxide content observed in the ceramics serves as evidence of the diverse calx recipes used, further reinforcing the notion of a dynamic and experimental phase in ceramic production during this period in Egypt (see Section 2.1; see also, Matin 2019: 1160). In contrast, glazes associated with the whiter, finer, and harder stonepaste bodies are colourless and transparent containing approximately 28–35 wt% PbO and 6–8 wt% $Na_2O + K_2O$ (Matin and Ownby 2023).

4.2.2 Fustat Fatimid Sgraffito (FFS)

Although a confusing label, the term FFS is used in the literature to refer to incised and carved stonepaste wares representing use of monochrome glazes (Bongianino 2014). Until the comprehensive work by Bongianino (2014, 2015, 2017), there has been limited research on this common type of pottery in Egypt. It appears that FFS were produced in response to the high demand for imported Chinese celadons and porcelains in Fatimid Egypt. The potters developed white stonepaste bodies with visible incisions and carvings, covered by a thin transparent glaze. These ceramics provided affordable alternatives in a similar style, incorporating Chinese elements while also offering a fresh interpretation within the FFS tradition (Bongianino 2014: 40–45). The range of stonepaste bodies appear similar to those of lustrewares although sherds of FFS have been analysed only sporadically and a more comprehensive study is necessary to comprehend the full range of variations. The composition of the glazes is similar to transparent glazes of lustrewares and the most common colours are honey/brown by iron oxide, green by copper oxide, and blue by cobalt oxide (Matin and Ownby 2023).

4.3 Syrian Stonepaste Wares

Syrian stonepaste gained recognition after it reached the European art market in the late nineteenth century. However, it was not until the Danish excavations in Hama in the first half of the twentieth century that more variations in Syrian stonepaste pottery were acknowledged (Poulsen 1957). Subsequent excavations conducted in several sites across the Euphrates region, spanning from southern Anatolia (e.g., Samsat (Redford 1995); Antioch (Waagé 1948)) and Syria (e.g., al-Raqqa (Sauvaget 1948); Qasr al-Hayr al-Sharqi (Grabar et al. 1978); Rusafa (Logar 1995); Tell Shahin (Tonghini 1995); Qal'at Ja'bar (Tonghini 1998)) to northern Iraq (e.g., 'Ana (Northedge et al. 1988)), have contributed to a better understanding of Syrian stonepaste production. The earliest form of stonepaste in Syria is identified through incised and carved techniques, while the introduction of lustre-decorated stonepaste seems to have occurred later. Further evidence is however needed to confirm this. Based on our current understanding, four main types of glazed stonepaste pottery are recognised in Syria.

4.3.1 Tell Minis Ware

'Tell Minis' ware represents the earliest production of stonepaste in Syria and is known in western literature after a village in north-west Syria where an assemblage of pottery was claimed to have been recovered and offered to the British Museum (acquired by the Victoria and Albert Museum and the David Collection; see Porter and Watson 1987). It is characterised by its remarkable thinness and fineness and its white, compact stonepaste body. It appears to be the product of the eleventh and first half of the twelfth century and has been found in excavations at several sites across the Euphrates (for a review see Tonghini 1998: 42–43) as well as various public and private collections.

Analysis of Tell Minis wares from Qal'at Ja'bar indicates that the stonepaste bodies are as expected made mainly of silica at around 85 wt% SiO_2. The chemical composition includes 5–7 wt% Al_2O_3, 2–5 wt% $Na_2O + K_2O$, and only minor (0.9–3.5 wt%) CaO which represents the nature of the clay used. The wares are decorated with one of the three techniques each with or without incised and carved motifs: monochrome glazed, in-glaze painted, or lustre decorated. The glazes are of the lead-alkali type including 18–30 wt% PbO and 10–15 wt% $Na_2O + K_2O$ (Tonghini 1998: 91). Most glazes are transparent, but Porter and Watson (1987: 181) reported that some lustre glazes were opacified by tin oxide and noted one non-lustred turquoise glaze that was tin-opacified. Monochrome glazes and the glazes associated with lustrewares can be either colourless or coloured. Turquoise colour is achieved by adding 1–3 wt% CuO, blue by 0.4–1.5 wt% CoO, and purple by adding as high as 20 wt% MnO. The polychrome in-glaze painted wares are similarly blue, turquoise, or purple, and always applied to a colourless glaze. For the lustre-decorated wares, the lustre survives only in traces and is typically of a pale gold-green colour with green tint (Tonghini 1998: 39, 91).

Laqabi Wares

A variation of the polychrome painted wares is the *laqabi* ware which is character-ised by its carved or deep incision decoration, painted in splashes of glazes of different colours under a transparent glaze (Mason 2004). The glaze has a tendency to run. Typical colours include cobalt blue, copper turquoise and green, manganese purple and iron yellow. In terms of quality, styles and chemical composition of the glaze (11–22 wt% PbO, 10–11 wt% $Na_2O + K_2O$ based on analysis of three samples by Mason 2004), *laqabi* wares are categorised as a type of Tell Minis ware group (or occasionally the Intermediate ware group (Section 4.2.2)). However, these wares were previously believed to originate from Iran, and only recent research on Syrian wares in the past few decades has uncovered evidence of Syrian production (see e.g., Tonghini 1998: 39).

4.3.2 Intermediate Ware

While chemically and petrographically similar to Tell-Minis ware, the Intermediate wares represent the more friable body and coarser quality of Raqqa wares to the extent that the two types are visually indistinguishable and can be differentiated only based on laboratory examination (see Tonghini 1998: 42; 'Related wares' in Porter and Watson 1987: 186; 'Groupe intemediare' in Poulsen 1957). Chronologically, it appears that the Intermediate ware overlapped Tell-Minis wares (or were introduced shortly after) but were produced for a longer period and ceased only shortly after the production of Raqqa wares. Tonghini (1998: 46) suggested that potters may have turned to producing Intermediate wares as a response to the marked rising-demand for stonepaste pottery. Their focus may have been more on increasing production rates or minimising fuel costs by firing wares at lower temperatures, rather than prioritising quality.

4.3.3 Raqqa Ware

The most widely discussed type of stonepaste pottery from Syria, the so-called 'Raqqa wares' reached the European Art market in the late nineteenth century and were labelled after their most probable provenance. Later archaeological excavations showed that Raqqa was indeed a ceramic pro-duction centre but that the so-called Raqqa wares were also produced at a number of other sites across the upper Euphrates and probably in other areas of Syria, such as Damascus (Tonghini 1998: 50; Jenkins-Madina 2006). On the basis of historical and stratigraphic evidence, the production of Raqqa wares began in the second half of the twelfth century and had fully devel-oped by the thirteenth century. Tonghini (1998: 49) suggested that while certain kilns seem to have been destroyed during the Mongol invasions of the thirteenth century, other production centres continued to function but eventually by the fourteenth century Raqqa wares had completely disappeared. Compared to Tell-Minis and Intermediate wares, Raqqa wares were more widely distributed across and beyond the Levant region. This was likely due in part to the prosperous economy of the Ayyubid period and the expansion of trade routes.

Raqqa wares are characterised by their rather rough, friable and porous bodies which stands in contrast with the dense and hard bodies of the preceding Tell Minis wares. Visual examination and chemical analysis of Raqqa wares from Qal'at Ja'bar indicate that the stonepaste bodies are made predominantly of quartz at around 82–90 wt% SiO_2 with very low amounts of clay indicated by 3–5 wt% CaO, 1.5–4 wt% MgO, and 2–4 wt% Al_2O_3. The $Na_2O + K_2O$ contents range between 2 and 5 wt% (Tonghini 1998: 90). Chemical analyses of a set of sixty-eight samples of Raqqa stonepaste from museum collections by Smith (2006) suggested a typical composition of 75 wt% SiO_2, 2–5 wt% Al_2O_3, and just over 3 wt% Na_2O. Only a sub-group of seven objects represented higher silica contents at approximately 80 wt% SiO_2.

The range of decorations varies from plain monochrome glazed to lusterwares. Raqqa wares also encompass a range of underglaze decoration techniques characterised by direct painting on the body, followed by the application of a colourless or coloured (turquoise, blue, or purple) transparent glaze (as discussed in Section 2.4.3). These include black-painted decoration under a transparent turquoise glaze, as well as black or black-and-blue painted designs under a transparent glaze. Polychrome underglaze-painted wares, often referred to as 'Rusafa wares', derive their name from the city located southwest of Raqqa. However, there is currently no evidence to designate Rusafa as the production centre for Syrian polychrome underglaze wares. These wares feature a variety of pigment colours including black, blue, turquoise, red, or purple, and exhibit significant figural and motif similarities with Persian polychrome overglaze enamel *mina'i* wares (Tonghini 1994: 254; Watson 2004: 294; see Section 5.2.5). They appear to have played a crucial role in the transmission of figural arts as well as coloured pigments between Iran and Anatolia during the twelfth/ thirteenth centuries (see also Section 5).

The transparent glazes associated with the plain monochrome, lustre, and underglaze-painted wares are of the alkali-lime compositional type (14–22 wt% $Na_2O + K_2O$). The plain monochrome glazes are either colourless, coloured turquoise by approximately 1–3 wt% CuO, blue by 0.7–0.9 wt% CoO, or purple by 4–6 wt% MnO. The most common underglaze-painted decoration was black achieved from chromium-based spinels (Franchi et al. 1995: 203). The black paint was sometimes paired with copper-based turquoise or cobalt-based blue underglaze painting. Red underglaze painting from bole pigments (a mixture of haematite and quartz; comparable to the one used on later Iznik wares discussed in Section 6.5) or dark red/purple from manganese oxide was added to this palette (Soustiel 1985: 118). Raqqa lustrewares may also show underglaze painting in blue or turquoise, as also seen on Persian and occasionally Egyptian lustrewares. The lustre decoration represents a characteristic chocolate brown colour achieved my mixed copper and silver salts. Again, the glaze-body interaction layer, predominantly quartz and cristobalite, as well as some pyroxenes were found (Pradell et al. 2008: 2655).

4.3.4 Mamluk Ware

This type of stonepaste pottery represents the Mamluk period and was manufactured at least from the late thirteenth to fifteenth centuries. Mamluk wares are sometimes referred to as 'Syrio-Egyptian' as they were produced both in Syria and Egypt. Production workshops were found in Damascus and Fustat, and it is possible that other centres existed. Mamluk wares were widely distributed across Syria, Jordan, Palestine, although rarely found in Northern Syria. Tonghini (1998: 54) suggested that this scarcity may be attributed to the region's low occupation after the Mongol invasion. They were also widely distributed in Europe perhaps as a result of the extensive network of trade facilitated by the Portuguese, Spanish, and Italian ships that sailed between North Africa and Europe.

Mamluk wares are characterised by their fine-grained, gritty, and porous stonepaste bodies. It appears that uncrushed rounded quartz was used together with crushed quartz (Tonghini 1998: 51) but petrographic analysis distinguishing different type of body fabrics have not been conducted. Based on analysis of Mamluk wares from Qal'at Ja'bar the bodies consist of 84–89 wt% SiO_2, and a predominantly calcareous clay represented by 6–8 wt% CaO. Compared to the preceding Syrian stonepaste wares, the Mamluk wares contain lower amounts of alkalis at around 2–3 wt % $Na_2O + K_2O$ (Tonghini 1998: 90).

The colourless, transparent glaze is often thickly applied and occasionally exhibits a green tint. The wares are either underglaze-painted with black and sometimes black and blue pigments from chromium spinels and cobalt oxides, respectively. Chemical analysis of glazes from Qal'at Ja'bar indicates that they are of the alkali-lime compositional type with approximately 17–19 wt% $Na_2O + K_2O$ (Tonghini 1998: 90).

5 Iran and the Greater Iran

Iran and the Greater Iran, also commonly referred to as the Persianate World, refers to lands spanning the area from Iraq to Central Asia as far as Uzbekistan and Tajikistan, where historically the Persian cultures and languages have thrived. The early development of Iranian pottery during the Islamic period can be traced in the southern Mesopotamia region, covering parts of Iraq and southwestern Iran. As discussed in Section 3, the prevalence of monochrome green- and turquoise-glazed jars (Section 3.2.1) was notable in the early Islamic archaeological layers in southwestern Iran. The development of Samarra-type pottery emphasised the significance of the assemblage in Susa (Section 3.2.3) in the Khuzestan province of Iran. Archaeological excavations have shown production of local copies of opaque-white wares and some other varieties of the Samarra-type pottery across the Iranian world. These local copies represent coarser and grittier products (see, e.g., Mason and Tite 1997). Most notable is the evidence of production, such as kilns, and wasters excavated in Siraf (Whitehouse 1979, 1972), an entrepôt on the east coast of the Persian Gulf, as well as in Sirjan in the Kirman province in central Iran (Morgan and Leatherby 1971; Williamson 1971).

But the first and most Iranian innovation in ceramic technology took place with the slip-painted wares of the Samanid period (819–999) in Eastern Iran. These glazed ceramics brought innovation in various aspects, introducing new forms and designs, using novel mineral pigments, such as chromite, and showcasing the masterful skills of potters in working with pigments under lead glazes (Section 5.1).

The beginning of stonepaste bodies in the eleventh or twelfth century marked a significant shift in the production of fine pottery in Iran (see Rugiadi 2016: 184). In Kashan, it was on these stonepaste bodies that lustre decoration achieved its utmost excellence and the new techniques of enamelled *mina'i* decoration and underglaze-painted decoration were executed. The Mongol invasions of Iran (1218–1257) temporarily halted production for a few decades, but Kashan resumed its ceramic production thereafter under the new Mongol Ilkhanid dynasty (1256–1335). In terms of style, Chinese designs became prevalent, featuring lotuses, peonies, dragons, phoenixes, and cloud bands. In addition, imported Chinese ceramics, especially celadons produced in the Longquan kilns during the Southern Song (1127–1279) and Yuan (1279–1368) dynasties, were locally copied in Iran on stonepaste bodies.

Limited information is available about ceramic production during the period between the collapse of the Ilkhanids in 1335 and the establishment of the Timurids (1370–1507) towards the close of the fourteenth century. Although fine ceramics from Kashan had previously gained widespread popularity across Iran and the broader Islamic world, reaching as far as Syria and Egypt, it seems that during this interval, potters might have relocated from Kashan to establish new workshops. This is evident in the production of the so-called 'Sultanabad' type underglaze-painted wares, which were produced in various centres, both within and outside Iran, closely imitating Iranian styles.

The most noteworthy ceramic development in the fourteenth century was the emergence of blue-and-white wares (Section 5.2.4). These wares reflect technological exchanges between Iran and China, both of which were under the umbrella of the Mongol Empire during this period. The Yuan Dynasty in China and the Ilkhanids in Iran, both ruled by descendants of Genghis Khan, played pivotal roles in this interchange. Chinese blue-and-white porcelain production was initially geared towards export to the Middle East, with little evidence of substantial domestic consumption during this time. However, in the ensuing centuries, these wares profoundly influenced global ceramic development in East and West Asia, as well as across Europe. They were widely exported and imitated throughout these regions. The earliest Persian imitations of Chinese blue-and-white wares, adopting a chinoiserie style, began during the Timurid period and persisted and improved throughout the Safavid era (1501–1736).

5.1 Clay-Bodied Ceramics

While the Abbasid Caliphate held sway during the ninth century CE, the region of Eastern Iran and Central Asia was effectively administered by local Persian elites. Consequently, local dynasties began to rise in prominence, gradually asserting their autonomy from the caliphate. Notable among these were the Tahirids (821–873), Saffarids (861–1003), and Samanids (819–999). The Samanids eventually emerged as the predominant power, controlling extensive territories encompassing Khurasan, Gurgan, Sistan, as well as parts of present-day Afghanistan, Tajikistan, Uzbekistan, Turkmenistan, and Kazakhstan. Their capital in Bukhara became a centre of science and learning during their rule, leading to a period of significant literary and intellectual achievements (Frye 1975: 154). During the Samanid rule, the region experienced thriving economic conditions, marked by flourishing trade, manufacturing, and mining. It was during the Samanid rule that the first fine glazed ceramics in the region emerged.

The presence of kilns and evidence of ceramic production is abundant in Nishapur, Samarqand, and various other sites throughout Eastern Iran and Central Asia (Wilkinson 1959; Siméon 2012). The general kiln designs and the use of kiln rods for stacking vessels appear to be similar to those used in the western Islamic world and were likely transferred from there. However, the challenge lies in distinguishing between locally made ceramics and imported ones. The designs are often very similar, making it difficult to pinpoint their production sites. Recent archaeometric studies have contributed to identifying different types of slips and pigments used, but they are rarely definitively associated with specific production sites.

There seem to have been connections between ceramic production and silver production and mining in Eastern Iran and Central Asia. It is not uncommon to find that the designs of ceramics have their origins in metalwork, and the shapes and patterns of ceramics from this region also appear to be influenced by silverwork. Moreover, recent lead isotope analysis studies on the origin of the lead used in glazes in southern Kazakhstan have indicated that this lead might have been sourced from the silver mines in the Tianshan districts or possibly from the silver cupellation processes (Klesner et al. 2021: 36).

One notable characteristic of Eastern Iranian pottery was the exceptional craftsmanship of the potters in working with a lead glaze, in combination with a wide range of pigments. For instance, in the case of slip-painted wares, these pigments were intentionally kept immobile, while in the case of splashed slip-painted wares, they were encouraged to flow under the lead glaze.

5.1.1 Slip-Painted Wares

The peak of creative innovation, encompassing both designs and pottery-making techniques, emerges in the slip-painted wares of the tenth century. These slip-painted wares, found in Eastern Iran and Central Asia, are covered with a white slip (or occasionally black or red slip) and feature thick, solidly painted designs applied over this underlying slip, all covered with a transparent lead glaze. This method of decoration distinguishes them from splashed slip-painted ceramics (Section 5.1.2), where white slips cover the entire body, decorated with colour splashes and sometimes incisions carved through the slip into the clay-based body.

Slip-painted pottery is found in a range of designs and qualities, with higher-quality examples originating from Nishapur, Samarqand, and Tashkent. Recent archaeometric analyses of slip-painted wares from hitherto little-known sites for instance in Bust and Lashkar-i Bazar in Afghanistan by Gulmini et al. (2013), southern Kazakhstan by Klesner et al. (2019), and Termez (southern Uzbekistan) by Molera et al. (2020) and Martínez Ferreras et al. (2019) have expanded our views of their production in this region.

Slip-painted pottery presents several variations in its decoration. A type that has been particularly praised by collectors and museums were the white slip-painted wares, typically featuring epigraphic, animal, or abstract decorations primarily in black, although red is also occasionally used. These are often referred to as black on white wares. Occasionally, the colours are reversed, with the ware covered in a black slip and the decorations applied in white slip under a transparent glaze. Epigraphic wares with Kufic inscriptions, in particular, have garnered significant attention due to their elegant and modern designs. Other decorative styles involve the use of a variety of polychrome slips, yellow-staining black painted wares, and slip-painted imitations of Samarra-type pottery, especially lustre-imitation wares. These typically feature black, red, and/or olive-green decorations.

The production of slip-painted wares persisted, albeit with diminishing quality, during the eleventh and twelfth centuries. Concurrently, a series of sgraffito wares with incised patterns through a slip emerged across Iran and neighbouring regions in Northwestern Iran, extending eastwards into Afghanistan (see Section 4.1.2. for Egyptian and Syrian sgraffito wares). Common varieties include plain types featuring incised decoration through a white slip, occasionally decorated with copper oxide green decoration under a transparent lead glaze. Other types, displaying a more controlled use of colour, have been identified and named by dealers based on the towns where many were claimed to have been found, such as 'Garrus', 'Amol', and 'Aghkhand' wares.

Lead Glaze

Chemical analyses have indicated that the lead glaze used to cover slip-painted wares typically consisted of 55 wt% PbO, 38 wt% SiO_2, 2.5 wt% Al_2O_3, and 2 wt% $Na_2O + K_2O$ (see e.g., Klesner et al. 2021: 203; Molera et al. 2020: 6; Henshaw 2010: 135–136; Gulmini et al. 2013; Mason 2004). The lead glaze was usually colourless but was occasionally coloured amber by iron oxide or green by copper oxide.

White slip

Chemical analyses conducted thus far have identified three main types of white slips on slip-painted wares of Eastern Iran and Central Asia. The first type, primarily composed of quartz, was identified on sherds from Nishapur and Afrasiyab/Samarqand by Holakooei et al. (2019: 764), from Ashsiket, Kuva, and Tashkent by Henshaw (2010: 156, 208, 220), and from various sites in Southern Kazakhstan by Klesner et al. (2019). It was noted that in sherds from Nishapur and Samarqand, the quartz was accompanied by minor amounts of anatase (TiO_2), as reported by Holakooei et al. (2019: 764), while in sherds from

Ashsiket and Tashkent, it was associated with high-aluminium clay, as stated by Henshaw (2010: 156, 221).

The second type of white slip is made from dehydrated pyrophyllite ($Al_2Si_4O_{10}(OH)_2$) and was found in some of the sherds discovered in Nishapur, as noted by Holakooei et al. (2019: 764). The third type consists of high-aluminium clay (16–25 wt% Al_2O_3) and was identified in sherds from Termez, located in southern Uzbekistan, as reported by Molera et al. (2020: 6). Additionally, this type of high-aluminium clay slip was identified in slip-painted pottery of Lashkar-i Bazar and Bust in Ghaznavid Afghanistan, although with higher alumina content (22.6–33 wt% Al_2O_3) and 1.5–3 wt% TiO_2 (Gulmini et al. 2013: 577).

Biscuit Firing

The firing process for Eastern Iranian and Central Asian slip-painted wares exhibits several distinctive characteristics that strongly indicate a biscuit firing stage. Notably, some of the epigraphic slip-painted dishes are impressively large, with diameters expanding to 45 cm. These wares were completely coated with a wet slip. Handling such sizable pieces, applying pigments and coloured slips, and then glazing them would have posed significant challenges. Biscuit firing, in this context, provided stability to the pieces, simplifying subsequent stages of decoration and glazing.

This proposition is supported by microstructural evidence observed in slip-painted sherds from Termez in Uzbekistan (Molera et al. 2020: 5–6) and Ashsiket (Henshaw 2010: 156). These findings revealed two crucial points. First, the glaze contained no or very few undissolved inclusions. Second, no or very few air bubbles or crystals were developed at the interface between the slip and glaze layers. K-feldspars were, however, detected which were formed during cooling. These observations strongly indicate that, after the application of the white slip over the clay body, the vessels underwent a biscuit firing. Following this, the glaze was applied, and the wares underwent a second firing.

Black Pigment

Two main types of black pigments were identified. The first type involved manganese or a mixture of manganese-iron black pigments. This type was identified in sherds from Bust and Lashkar-i Bazar by Gulmini et al. (2013: 581), from Nishapur and Samarqand by Holakooei et al. (2019: 764) and Bouquillon et al. (2012, 116), from Termez by Molera et al. (2020, 6), from Ashsiket, Kuva, and Tashkent by Henshaw (2010, 141, 207, 219), and from various sites in southern Kazakhstan by Klesner et al. (2021: 16–17). It was found to be used either individually or in combination with chromite.

The second type was identified as chromite $(Mg,Fe)Cr_2O_4$, on sherds found in Nishapur (Holakooei et al. 2019: 768). Chromite was identified on all slip-painted wares with a red background slip, which is associated with iron-rich clay, and with polychrome decorations in black, yellow, white. Additionally, some of the slip-painted wares with polychrome decorations (black, red, yellow) on white slip featured chromite. Chromite black was also identified on three sherds from Bust and Lashakar-i Bazar of Ghaznavid Afghanistan (Gulmini et al. 2013: 581).

Moreover, chromite was identified in the *Yellow-staining black painted wares*, a type of slip-painted ware where the decoration, applied on the white slip, exhibits a black pigment that turns yellow in its surroundings (see e.g., Wilkinson 1973: 213–228). Klesner et al. (2021: 203) showed that the black pigment is a variety of magnesium aluminium chromite $(Fe,Mg)(Cr,Al)_2O_4$ with an average composition of 60 wt% Cr_2O_3, 20 wt% MgO, 13 wt% Al_2O_3, and 5 wt% FeO. This chromite pigment has been used in different proportions in different sites. Holakooei et al. (2019: 768) showed that the black pigment on wares found in Samarqand showed lower chromium contents and seemed to have been diluted as compared to those found in Nishapur. The yellow colour that emerges in the vicinity of the black pigment is produced as a result of Cr (and Fe) dissolving in the overlaying lead glaze during firing (see also, Henshaw 2010: 147).

The chromium-based technology producing yellow hues was also employed to create olive-green slips in some other types of slip-painted pottery. For instance, *Imitation lustrewares,* slip-painted wares imitating the designs on the Samarra-type lustrewares were produced in Samanid Eastern Iran using an olive-green slip (see Wilkinson 1973: 179–204), as well as in Ghaznavid Afghanistan (Gulmini et al. 2013: 584). The slip is composed of quartz, clay, as well as chromite particles. Similar to the yellow-staining black painted ware, the chromium would have dissolved within the glassy matrix of the overlying lead glaze during firing, resulting in a green/yellow colour. Holakooei et al. (2019: 768) also identified chrome yellow $PbCrO_4$ particles formed in some of the glazes from Samarqand as a result of the reaction between chromite and the lead glaze. In comparison to the yellow-staining black painted wares, the olive-green slips contain lower amounts of chromium, but they are applied more thickly, typically at approximately 50–100 µm (Henshaw 2010: 146; Holakooei et al. 2019: 768; Klesner et al. 2021: 203).

Furthermore, apart from imitation lustrewares, the olive-green slip was also used to paint other types of slip-painted wares. Chemical analysis revealed that some of these, found in sherds from Samarqand and Ashsiket, also contain copper (Holakooei et al. 2019; Henshaw 2010).

5.1.2 Splashed Slip-Painted Wares

Splashed slip-painted wares, along with buff wares (Section 5.1.3), constitute some of the largest pottery groups discovered in Nishapur and have also been unearthed in Samarqand and other locations in the Eastern Iranian and Central Asian region. These ceramics are distinguished by their white slip coating decorated with splashes of copper green, iron brown, and manganese black under a transparent lead-based glaze. A variant of this ware is further decorated with incised designs.

The general compositions of the high lead glaze and pigments are similar to those found on slip-painted wares. Holakoeei et al. (2019: 768) conducted an in-depth analysis of the manganese black pigment used in splashed wares from Nishapur and Samarqand. Based on the proportion of iron/manganese in the pigment, their findings suggest that the black pigment in the splashed wares was achieved using a manganese-rich mineral, with minimal iron content.

5.1.3 Buff Wares with Opaque Lead Stannate Yellow Decoration

Buff wares, named after the buff-coloured ceramic body, are a type of polychrome painted wares under a transparent lead glaze that became known following excavations conducted by the Metropolitan Museum of Art in Nishapur between 1935 and 1948 (Sardar 2015). They were the largest group of glazed pottery found in Nishapur (Wilkinson 1973: 3–53), but sherds of this type were also unearthed in Merv. A distinctive feature of buff wares is the prevalent use of lead-stannate opaque yellow pigment complemented by designs in black, green, and occasionally white slip, featuring geometric patterns or dense animated motifs. Iconographers have suggested that these animate motifs might represent local Persian festivities that had survived from the pre-Islamic Sasanian period. However, a more recent perspective by Siméon (2017) proposes that they may instead depict rituals conducted by the army of the Buyids, which was a Persian Shia dynasty that gained influence in the tenth century, primarily in the western part of the Samanid Empire, which ruled over a predominantly Sunni population.

The production technology of buff wares also appears to exhibit influences from the western regions. Their prevalent use of lead-stannate yellow pigment, deep bowl shapes, and certain geometric and animal figures bear a resemblance to the Yellow Glazed Family wares of Syria (Section 3.1.2). An analysis of the yellow decoration on a single shard of Nishapur buff ware by Mason (2004:

135, sherd ROM.20) revealed a composition of 59.0 wt% PbO, 34.8 wt% SiO_2, and 1.1 wt% SnO_2. Non-invasive analyses of three Nishapur buff ware sherds by Holakoeei et al. (2019: 766) confirmed the presence of lead-stannate ($PbSnO_3$) in the yellow as well as green pigments. Copper and iron were responsible for the green and red colours, respectively. A mixture of iron and manganese was used for black decorations (Holakoeei et al. 2019: 764).

5.1.4 Opaque Yellow Glazed Wares

The use of opaque yellow glaze was not unique to buffwares. Known as Opaque yellow glazed wares, these ceramics featured an opaque yellow glaze with green decoration. Wilkinson (1973: 205) documents their production and use in Nishapur during the ninth and tenth centuries, though production seems to have ceased thereafter. Chemical analysis of three sherds from Nishapur, four sherds from Takht-i Sulaiman, and one sherd from Merv indicate that the yellow glazes were of the high lead type with approximately 65 wt% PbO, 26 wt% SiO_2, and 4 wt% SnO_2, with Pb/Sn calx ratios ranging between 10.5–28.3. The microstructure shows a proliferation of lead stannate crystals throughout the glaze. However, the decorations on the Takht-i Sulaiman and Merv sherds may not strictly adhere to those of the Nishapur opaque yellow glazed wares. The Merv sherds feature brown decorations, while the Takht-i Sulaiman sherds exhibit brown and white decorations alongside yellow and green ones.

The red clay body, which appears similar to that used for slip-painted and splashed slip-painted wares of Nishapur, contain 7–16 wt% CaO and 2.5–5 wt% MgO and is of a highly immature fabric (Matin 2016: 69–76; Matin et al. 2018: 61–64).

5.1.5 Opaque White Glazed Wares

Little known and rarely discussed, the opaque glazed ceramics of Samarqand feature entirely distinct decorative styles when compared to the earlier Samarra-type ceramics. Covered with opaque white glaze, they are decorated with designs predominantly in green and occasionally in purple/brown. The opaque white glazes employed belong to the lead-alkali category and contain approximately 8–10 wt% $Na_2O+ K_2O$ and 15–19 wt% PbO (Matin et al. 2018). These glazes achieve their opacity through the inclusion of 3.4–6.1 wt% SnO_2 (Pb/Sn ratios ranging from 3.7 to 5), along with the presence of quartz particles and air bubbles (Matin et al. 2018: 61–64).

5.2 Stonepaste Ceramics

Unlike Egypt and Syria, where different stages of the development of stonepaste pottery are to some extent recognised, our understanding of early stonepaste production in Iran is limited. The technology of creating artificial siliceous stones has been a longstanding practice in Iran, as seen in the production of millstones (Mishmastnehi 2018) and the so-called Egyptian faience. However, there is currently no evidence indicating the early development of stonepaste technology in Iran.

The commonly accepted assumption is that the introduction of stonepaste in Iran, along with lustre technology, took place after the movement of potters from Egypt to Iran in the second half of the twelfth century, driven by the economic and political upheavals of the final years of the Fatimids. During this period, Iran was part of the Seljuq Empire, established in the eleventh century by the Seljuq Turks, nomadic Turkic people originating from Central Asia. Initially advancing into Khurasan, they established their capital in Nishapur but later extended their influence into the central Iran and relocated the capital to Isfahan.

Simultaneously, the Khwarazmian, another Turkic ruling dynasty, governed significant parts of Central Asia and Iran starting around the eleventh century. Eventually overcoming the Seljuqs, they achieved independence in 1190 CE. Subsequently, the Mongols, led by Genghis Khan, invaded the Khwarazmian territory in 1219. The early development of stonepaste occurred in the pre-Mongol period, and while technological and stylistic changes may not align precisely with major historical events, the overall period witnessed significant innovations in ceramics technology.

Simple types of stonepaste with monochrome glazes featuring incised, carved, or moulded decorations were manufactured at various sites across the Iranian world. Perhaps a more significant innovation during the twelfth and thirteenth centuries was the introduction of underglaze-painted wares, which originated in the decades preceding the Mongol invasions of Iran. A precursor to these is considered to be the 'silhouette' ware, distinguished by the application of a black slip made of a combination of chromite and quartz under a transparent turquoise glaze on a stonepaste body (Mason et al. 2001). The best-known true early underglaze-painted wares of the thirteenth century are characterised by painting with a black chromite pigment under an alkali-lime turquoise copper-based glaze (see Figure 8; see also, Mason et al. 2001; Aarab et al. 2025). Blue, turquoise, and purple underglaze paintings were also applied under transparent turquoise or colourless glazes. Over time, these were succeeded by the fine-quality 'Sultanabad'-type wares of the Ilkhanid period with decoration in low relief in a white slip against a pale grey background. Further development of the underglaze technique in the form of underglaze blue-painted wares marked a turning point as discussed in Section 5.2.4.

Finer, luxurious types of stonepaste with lustre or *mina'i* decoration are dated to at least the late twelfth century based on their inscriptions – the earliest dated lustre piece is inscribed 1179 (Watson 1976: 8), and the earliest *mina'i* is inscribed 1180 (Watson 1994: 171). Various sites have been speculated as the production site for the lustre and *mina'i* wares, but there is a range of evidence that the main – and perhaps single – production centre was Kashan, though the possibility of other sites cannot be entirely ruled out.

Literary sources suggest Kashan's renown in ceramic production, and it is believed that the Persian word for tile, *qashi* or *kashi*, is derived from this town's name. Various kilns and wasters from different wares have been discovered in Kashan, although those related specifically to lustre and *mina'i* wares are yet to be found (see Akbari 2019). Signed works of potters often carry inscriptions directly referencing Kashan. Among the various recorded potters, two prominent masters stand out: Abu Zaid, mentioned on both lustre and *mina'i* pieces (Watson 1994), and Mohammad bin Abi Tahir, a member of the Abu Tahir family with generations of pottery work in Kashan. Abu'l Qasim, a grandson of Mohammad, transitioned to become a historian in the Mongol court, leaving behind a treatise in Persian on the production of ceramics and lustre wares. The earliest known manuscript dates to 1301 CE, and clearly states that at time of the manuscript, the production of *mina'i* wares (referred to as *haft-rang* in the source) were ceased but that the *lajvardina* types were still being produced. The manuscript is an invaluable source for the study of the processes of production, the sources of raw materials, as well as recipes for stonepaste bodies, glazes, and various types of decoration. An English translation and discussion of these are given by Allan 1973 and Matin 2020.

The recipe given by Abu'l Qasim Kashani for stonepaste suggests that it was made of 80% siliceous stones (mainly quartz/quartzite), 10% white plastic clay and 10% of frit glass. Chemical analyses, consistent with this recipe, have indicated a typical composition of stonepaste bodies for lustre (Kingery and Vandiver 1986; Pradell et al. 2008), *mina'i* (Mason et al. 2001; Mason 2004), and *lajvardina* (Osete-Cortina et al. 2010; Röhrs et al. 2022) wares. This composition is mainly composed of 85 wt% SiO_2, 6.5 wt% Al_2O_3, 1.5 wt% CaO, and 5 wt% $Na_2O + K_2O$. However, the differences in their microstructure and firing temperatures only have been studied to a limited extent.

5.2.1 Lustre Ware

Three styles of Kashan lustre ware have been identified by Watson (1985a, 1976) which appear to indicate the stages of its development. The earliest stage appears to be the 'monumental style' where the main figures were depicted in reverse, that is, instead of painting the main motifs in lustre, they were left white against a lustre background. Rather distinct from this style is the 'miniature style' with designs which as the name suggests were closely related to the manuscript illumination of the period, which is missing, but is seen to a large extent in the later manuscripts of fourteenth and fifteenth centuries. Watson (1976) has suggested that the 'miniature style', which is painted in lustre on a white background, was most probably developed primarily for the enamelled *mina'i* wares (Section 5.2.2). Finally, the 'Kashan' style, with designs in reverse on a lustre ground appeared to have been an amalgamation of the two styles (see, e.g., Figure 10a).

The glazes were of two compositional types: lead-alkali type (12–24 wt% PbO, 5–13 wt% $Na_2O + K_2O$) opacified by typically 3.5–8 wt% SnO_2 (see, e. g., Figure 10b), and a soda-lime transparent type (17–20 wt% $Na_2O + K_2O$) (Kingery and Vandiver 1986: 116; Mason 2004; Pradell et al. 2008). It appears that the soda-lime glazes were often used to glaze the reverse of dishes and interior of the closed vessels. The lustre layers appear to be a mixture of copper (2–5 wt% Cu) and silver (<5 wt% Ag), with copper contents significantly higher than those of Egyptian Fatimid lustres (Pradell et al. 2008: 2661; see also Section 5.1.3).

(a)   (b)

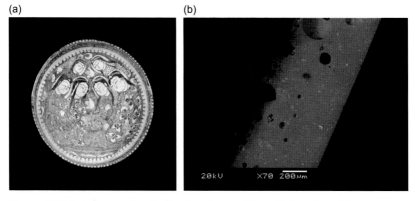

Figure 10 (a) An example of a Kashan Lustre Ware (Ashmolean Museum, acc. no. EA1956.33), (b) a typical backscattered SEM photomicrograph of a section through opaque white glaze (lead-alkali compositional type) into stonepaste body of a Kashan lustre ware.

5.2.2 Mina'i *Ware*

The Persian term *mina'i*, adopted by dealers and collectors since the twentieth century, refers to overglaze enamelled ceramics from medieval Iran. In this technique, once the glazed vessel was fired it was painted with various enamels and fired for the second time. The second firing was performed at lower temperatures than the first, preventing the underlying glaze from softening, while still high enough to allow the enamels to fuse. *Mina'i* wares feature figural representations closely tied to contemporary Persian manuscript painting, even though the manuscripts themselves have not survived. They also feature geometric, floral, and epigraphic designs, coming in various sizes and shapes of vessel, with bowls being the most common. Due to the popularity of *mina'i* wares in the art market during the 1930s, unscrupulous dealers went to great lengths to assemble new complete vessels from unrelated sherds. They concealed these efforts through intensive overpainting and restoration. Therefore, caution is needed when dealing with museum complete pieces (see e.g., Norris and Watson 2021; Watson 1985b).

There seem to have been close connections between *mina'i* and lustre production, and pieces with both lustre and enamel decorations represent complex production processes (McClary 2022). Kashan stands out as the most convincing centre for its production. Based on inscriptions on known pieces, *mina'i* wares was produced between 1180 and 1219 (Watson 1994: 171). However, there are suggestions that the chronology needs to be reconsidered based on evidence of *mina'i* tiles in Konya dated as early as 1174 (McClary 2016). Abu'l Qasim Kashani, in his 1301 CE treatise, asserts that this technique, referred to as *haft-rang* [seven-coloured], had ceased to be practiced. Recent evidence of *mina'i*-decorated sherds, identified as the Fatimid Fustat Sgraffito type based on the foot shapes and glazing manner, as presented by Watson (2024), suggests that the *mina'i* technique may have travelled westward to Fustat. Additionally, it may have served as inspiration for figural images and motifs on Syrian Rusafa wares (see Section 4.3.3).

The base glazes are of the lead-alkali compositional type (14–22 wt% PbO and 7–12 wt% $Na_2O + K_2O$) and opacified by 6–10 wt% SnO_2 (see Figure 7). They are either white or coloured turquoise by addition of 1–2 wt% CuO as colorant (Mason et al. 2001; Mason 2004: Table 6.5; Wen and Pollard 2014).

In some cases, applied relief with a composition similar to the stonepaste body was added over the base glaze. Cut gold leaf gilding was also sometimes applied using an organic binder after the first firing, before any of the enamels were applied. SEM microstructures often reveal bubbles under the gold leaf, likely caused by the burning of organic binders during the second firing (Holakooei et al. 2023).

A wide range of colour decorations are used on *mina'i* wares. Koss et al. (2009), in their chemical and microstructural analysis of a set of *mina'i* sherds, highlighted the presence of a range, rather than a singular *mina'i* technology. Notable variations in enamel compositions, the sequence of application, and firing regimes are evidence of this range, often correlating with stylistic distinctions.

Based on their microstructural studies, most enamel layers exhibit an even linear interface, with minimal interaction with the underlaying base glaze. This suggests that these enamels were likely applied after the initial firing. However, turquoise glaze, as well as certain varieties of blue and purple, appear to have been applied as an inglaze over the raw base glaze before firing.

Turquoise glaze was achieved by 1–2 wt% copper oxide. A range of blue were obtained by 0.1–6.5 wt% CoO, accompanied by 0.3–2.1 wt% FeO and 0.6–5.3 wt% As_2O_3. These blues vary in microstructure, chemistry, appearance, intensity of colours, and ways of application and have been categorised to different types by Koss et al. (2009) and Wen and Pollard (2014). Based on their analyses it appears that in some cases, the cobalt pigment was mixed with a mixture similar to that of the base glaze powder and applied, while in others, the cobalt pigment was processed into a frit (see also, Mason et al. 2001).

The main black pigment used on *mina'i* wares was chromite containing 1.2–4 wt% Cr_2O_3, accompanied by 0.6–3.6 wt% FeO and 1.2–3 wt% MgO. This pigment was used for drawings under the base glaze, as well as opaque, dense accent areas (such as facial features and hair), although the chromite used is more finely ground in the former case which allows for finer and thinner application of underdrawings. Another type of black was achieved by a mixture of manganese and iron oxides (0.5–6.5 wt% MnO and 3–8.1 wt% FeO).

The red pigment consisted of iron oxide (2.5–8.5 wt% FeO), sourced from hematite, and the pink appears to be a mixture of hematite and tin oxide (1.2 wt% FeO and 4.7 wt% SnO_2). The purple was achieved by manganese oxide (1–3 wt% MnO), and olive-green type with mottled yellow was found to consist of chromium, iron, and copper, although the specific chemical composition was not provided (see Koss et al. 2009: 43).

The archaeometric examination of pigments indicates a strikingly similar use of chromium-based pigments on *mina'i* wares as seen in earlier slip-painted wares from Eastern Iran. The use of chromite pigment for black and the identification of chromium in an olive-green pigment with mottled yellow on *mina'i* wares closely parallel the practices developed by earlier potters in Eastern Iran. Abu'l Qasim Kashani, in his treatise, mentioned that the chromite, known as *muzarrad* in medieval Persian, was procured from the mountains of Jajarm in Khurasan, Northeastern Iran. While it remains uncertain whether this was also the source for the chromium-based pigments in slip-painted wares, the fact that the mine(s) were situated in a similar region raises an intriguing possibility linked to the initial use of these pigments in Eastern Iranian wares.

The connections between *mina'i* and slip-painted wares extend beyond the use of chromite pigments; stylistic parallels are also apparent. Both feature epigraphic decorations around the rim and showcase large sizes, reaching up to approximately 50 cm in diameter. These shared characteristics suggest a continuity and further development of technologies and styles initially employed in Samanid wares, evolving into the twelfth-century Seljuq wares.

5.2.3 Lajvardina Ware

Lajvardina wares, adapted from *mina'i* ceramics, were produced during the thirteenth and fourteenth centuries within the Ilkhanid Period in Iran. The designs are non-figural, typically featuring geometric patterns. Reflecting the influence of the Mongol period in Iran, Chinese motifs such as phoenixes, lotuses, and peonies are commonly seen particularly on *lajvardina* tiles. These tiles were extensively used at Takht-i Sulaiman in northwestern Iran, serving as the summer palace for Abaqa Khan, the grandson of Ghengis Khan and the second Ilkhanid ruler. It appears that potters from Kashan were brought to the site to produce these tiles (Masuya 1997: 226).

Chemical analyses of *lajvardina* sherds from Takht-i Sulaiman, Sultaniya, Rayy, Yazd, and Kashan indicated that base glazes come in blue, achieved with 0.3–0.8 wt% CoO, accompanied by 0.3–1.2 wt% As_2O_3 and 1–2.3 wt% FeO), or turquoise, achieved with 1.4–3.2 wt% CuO. White base glazes, which from the data currently available, appear to be exclusive to *lajvardina* sherds from Takht-i Sulaiman, are achieved with 1.2–8.9 wt% SnO_2 (Holakooei et al. 2023).

The glazes fall into three main compositional types: lead-alkali (8–38 wt% PbO and 10–14 wt% $Na_2O + K_2O$) opacified by 5–11 wt% SnO_2, or alkali-lime (4–26 wt% $Na_2O + K_2O$; 2–8 wt% CaO) without opacification (Osete-Cortina et al. 2010; Röhrs et al. 2022; Holakooei et al. 2023). Additionally, one sample appear to belong to the low lead-alkali compositional type (4 wt% PbO; 3.5 wt% K_2O, and unspecified levels of Na_2O), with 1.2 wt% SnO_2. The main distinguishing factor between glaze compositions is the presence or absence of lead-tin calx for opacification, categorising the final glaze composition as either (low) lead-alkali or alkali-lime. Based on analysed sherds, all turquoise base glazes fall under the lead-alkali type, blue glazes fall under both lead-alkali and alkali-lime, and white base glazes exhibit all three compositional types.

The gilding, along with the black, white, red enamels, and blue and turquoise inglazes, are similar to those observed on *mina'i* wares. Black enamels employed either chromite or manganese oxide. Analysis of chromite black pigments on sherds from Takht-i Sulaiman identified chromium and iron, but no manganese, indicating the sole use of iron-chromite. Tin oxide and iron oxide (from hematite) were used for white and red enamels, respectively. Similar to the *mina'i* wares, chromium-based olive green/yellow were also identified on *lajvardina* sherds from Takht-i Sulaiman and $PbCrO_4$ was also identified. Cobalt and copper oxides were introduced for blue and turquoise inglaze decorations respectively.

5.2.4 Interactions with China – Underglaze Blue-Painted Wares

At the core of the development of blue-and-white wares were two pivotal technologies that found their way from Iran to China. The first was the underglaze painting technology, and the second involved the use of cobalt blue pigment, specifically sourced from the cobalt mine in the village of Qamsar, situated southwest of Kashan (Matin and Pollard 2015, 2017). These two technologies converged in Jingdezhen, in eastern China, during the second quarter of the fourteenth century, giving rise to the production of exquisite porcelain ware with underglaze cobalt blue painting. Watson (2020: 347) draws attention to discarded pieces of early Yuan Chinese Blue-and-white porcelain bearing Persian verses, supposedly inscribed by a native Persian, as evidence supporting the idea that these techniques were transferred through direct personal contact.

The earliest Persian Chinoiserie underglaze blue-painted copies seem to have originated in Samarqand, potentially produced by potters forced to relocate from Iran and Syria to Samarqand by Timur (see, e.g., Watson 1987). Mason (1996: 35, 112, 114) argues that the execution and motifs of these wares appears to follow imitations of blue-and-white Yuan porcelain excavated at Hama and Fustat. It appears, however, that the Syrian potters working in Samarqand would have needed to experiment with locally available materials, resulting in discernibly different stonepaste body fabrics from those in Syria. Nevertheless, they did share the use of quartz sand, as opposed to crushed quartz (Mason 1996: 35).

It appears that potters subsequently began to migrate from Samarqand westwards and established workshops in cities like Nishapur, Mashhad, Tabriz, and others. Mason (1996) proposed various petrofabric groups based on petrographic analysis of samples tentatively or securely associated with these cities. Subsequently, Tite et al. (2011) conducted chemical analyses to determine the composition of their stonepaste bodies. For instance, the 'Nishapur petrofabric' group, as identified by Mason (1996: 38, 42), included wasters and pottery from the kiln site at Nishapur, along with a dish inscribed with its place of manufacture as Nishapur. Chemical analysis by Tite et al. (2011, 572) indicated that the stonepaste body consisted of 92 wt% SiO_2, 3 wt% Al_2O_3, 1.5 wt% CaO, and 2 wt% $Na_2O + K_2O$.

A crucial aspect in the production of both Chinese Blue-and-white porcelain and their Persian imitations was the acquisition and use of cobalt blue pigment. The cobalt mine in Kashan is well-documented in Persian and Chinese historical manuscripts (for a review of Persian sources see Matin and Pollard 2015; for Chinese sources see Watt 1979 and Wen 2012: 70–130), and surveys, along with chemical and mineralogical analyses of its ore (Matin and Pollard 2017). It has been established that the cobalt ores from Kashan were of the high arsenic type, often accompanied by other high-iron minerals. The presence of arsenic and iron alongside cobalt in the analysis of cobalt pigments serves as a distinctive fingerprint indicating the source as the Kashan mine. Extensive analyses of Chinese blue-and-white porcelain, as well as Persian and other Islamic imitations, have revealed that the Kashan mine was the sole source of cobalt used in Chinese blue-and-white porcelain during the Yuan and early Ming dynasties. The fate of Kashan cobalt in China beyond this period remains unclear, and it is uncertain whether it was combined with other sources or entirely replaced by Chinese local sources. In Iran, while cobalt blue was used in the pre-Mongol period, its prominence increased significantly after the Mongol invasions. It became a dominant secondary colour on lustrewares, the primary glaze colour in *lajvardina* wares and subsequently featured in the underglaze blue-painted wares of the Timurid and Safavid periods. Chemical analyses conducted by Wen (2012: 305–336) on a wide range of Islamic glazed wares indicate that cobalt from the Kashan mine continued to be used for much longer, persisting until the nineteenth century, not only in Iran but also across the Islamic world. One notable exception seems to be the ceramics of the Iznik type (Section 6.5), which, based on its chemical composition, appear to have employed cobalt from a different source.

6 Anatolia

Anatolia, the present-day Turkey, had been a core territory of the Byzantine Empire since the decline of the Roman Empire. However, starting in the eleventh century CE, a combination of internal weaknesses within the Empire, such as political instability and economic difficulties, and external pressures from the Seljuq Turks contributed to the Empire's decline in

Anatolia. With the presence of Seljuqs in Iran and Central Asia, as discussed in Section 6, a branch migrated to Anatolia in the eleventh century CE, and established the Seljuqs of Rum, bringing with them new technologies and decorative styles. Under their sultans, they established the Sultanate of Rum, which covered significant portion of the Central and Western Anatolian region. This migration and the Sultanate's establishment left a profound and lasting impact in the region. The Seljuqs introduced their Islamic Turkic culture and tradition, as well as language, and gradually expanded their control, challenging Byzantine authority. This rise of the Seljuq Sultanate of Rum played a crucial role in shaping subsequent events until 1243 CE when the Mongols from Central Asia defeated the Seljuqs during the Battle of Kose Dag in Central Anatolia, marking a turning point in the history of the region.

During the subsequent Ilkhanid reign, the Mongol rule in Western Asia, began. The Seljuq Sultanate of Rum fell under political and economic control of the Ilkhanids, and the Seljuq authority progressively waned. Instead, various Turkish tribal leaders, known as bey, established their own beyliks and carved out territories in different parts of Anatolia. In the late thirteenth century CE, Osman I gradually emerged as the most powerful among the beyliks and founded the Ottoman Beylik. Under his leadership and that of his successors, the Ottoman Beylik expanded its territory and influence, and glazed Islamic ceramics became increasingly dominant over Byzantine ceramics across expanding areas of the region. Under the reign of the Ottoman Sultan Mehmed II, the conquest of Constantinople in 1453 CE marked the definitive end of the Byzantine Empire and the beginning of the Ottoman Empire.

Regarding ceramic production, there are, first, Seljuq ceramics (Section 6.1), followed by Beylik ceramics (Section 6.2). Then, at the beginning of the Ottoman period, there is the arrival in the 1410s of a group of potters from Iran who styled themselves the Masters of Tabriz (Section 6.3). Subsequently, by the mid-fifteenth century CE, Ottoman potters were producing Miletus ware (Section 6.4) and from the end of the fifteenth century onwards, the production of Iznik wares marked one of the technological and artistic peaks of Islamic ceramic production (Section 6.5).

6.1 Seljuq Ceramics

During the reign of Sultan Alaeddin Keykubad I (1220–37), and prior to their defeat by the Mongols in 1243 CE, the Seljuqs undertook many major building and infrastructure projects, including the Royal Palace at Konya and the palace of Kubad-Abad which is situated on the southwestern shore of Lake Beysehir in Central Turkey, about 100 km west of Konya. Although no inscription stating the construction date of the palace of Kubad-Abad has been found, a mosque inscription dated 1234 CE in the neighbouring village indicates that a considerable settlement developed around the complex at that time.

Freestone et al. (2009) have analysed some fifty tiles excavated from the palace of Kubad-Abad, and Öztürk et al. (2022) have analysed six tiles from excavation in Konya. The Kubad-Abad tiles were categorised into three basic forms: polychrome decorated eight-pointed star-shaped tiles, polychrome and bichrome decorated cross-shaped tiles, and monochrome turquoise blue rectangular tiles. Analytical data were also obtained for two contemporary ceramic vessels from the site.

The bodies of these Seljuq tiles are of the stonepaste type containing predominately angular quartz up to about 5 mm in diameter (85–93 wt% SiO_2). The absence of composite quartz-feldspar grains, plus the predominance of monocrystalline quartz, suggests that the quartz was obtained by crushing quartz pebbles. The high alumina contents (5–7 wt% Al_2O_3), together with the low lime (1–3 wt% CaO) and iron oxide contents (< 1 wt% Fe_2O_3), of both the tile and vessel bodies suggests the use of a kaolinitic clay, rather than a pale-firing calcareous clay, frequently used for stonepaste bodies. The quartz particles are bonded together by the addition of a soda-lime frit. The added frit content of the tiles, as reflected by their soda contents (0.7–1.8 wt% Na_2O), is lower than that of the Seljuq vessel bodies (2.4 wt% Na_2O). Since soda contents equal to or greater than 2 wt% are observed for most stonepaste vessel bodies, it seems possible that this reflects the greater strength required for vessels as compared to decorative tiles supported by their backing-wall. Both tin-opacified lead alkali glazes (13–15 wt% PbO, 9–13 wt% Na_2O, 5–8 wt% SnO_2) and transparent soda-lime glazes (11–15 wt% Na_2O, 3–7 wt% CaO) were used.

The colorants copper which is used to produce the monochrome turquoise (pale blue) glazed rectangular tiles, and manganese and cobalt which are used to produce purple and dark blue glazes, respectively. In addition, one group of tiles has a well-defined underglaze cobalt pigment, comprising fine particles of cobalt-bearing iron oxide mixed with fine quartz particles. This underglaze appears to be an attempt to stabilise or fix the cobalt pigment and to stop it from bleeding into the glaze.

The second particulate colorant is chromite which provides an underglaze black and which is widely used for borders and motifs to produce a silhouette-type decoration. The black chromite particles are a chrome-rich spinel composed mainly of Cr_2O_3, with subordinate Fe_2O_3, Al_2O_3, and MgO, in addition to variable amounts of copper oxide, absorbed from the copper colorant in the glaze (Section 2.4.2).

6.2 Beylik Ceramics

From about the mid-fourteenth century CE through to the early fifteenth century CE, Beylik potters in western Anatolia produced various types of pottery, including Polychrome Sgraffitto, Moulded ware (glazed and unglazed), and Monochrome Turquoise Glazed Wares (Burlot and Waksman 2021).

All three pottery types were made using a clay body which was dried before being coated with a clay-based slip, into which a pattern was incised in the case of Polychrome Sgraffitto ware, and the pottery was then biscuit-fired. After the biscuit-firing, additional decoration was sometime painted onto the slip before applying a glaze and firing for a second time.

In the case of Polychrome Sgraffitto and Moulded Wares, transparent high lead glazes (45–65 wt% PbO, < 2 wt% $Na_2O + K_2O$) were used. The glaze colorants used were iron yellow-brown, copper green and manganese purple for the dots on Polychrome Sgraffitto ware. Polychrome Sgraffitto Ware, but not Moulded Ware, was also used in the production of Late Byzantine tableware in, for example, Pergamon and Ephesus. Both Byzantine and Islamic tablewares were technically similar, using transparent high lead glazes, but stylistically different.

In contrast, the glazes applied to the Monochrome Turquoise Glazed ware are tin-opacified and of the lead-alkali type (27–37 wt% PbO, 3–8 wt% $Na_2O + K_2O$ with 8–11 wt% SnO_2). Therefore, these glazes are uniquely Islamic and differ from the glazes used by Byzantine potters, who did not produce ceramics with tin-opacified glaze. Because of the lower lead oxide content and the higher alkali content of this glaze, the copper colorant produced a turquoise colour, rather than the green colour observed in the previous high lead glazed wares.

The production of Monochrome Turquoise Glazed Wares is widespread in the Islamic world, including at Qal'at Ja'bar in Syria where it is again produced using a clay-based body (Section 4.1.4). However, in the absence of any comparable analytical data for the glaze, it is not possible to establish whether or not there are any technical links.

6.3 Masters of Tabriz Tiles

It has already been discussed in Section 6 that Timur forcibly relocated craftspeople from across his burgeoning empire to the capital Samarqand, where he commissioned the development of various crafts and undertook extensive architectural projects. Among these were a group of potters, who were originally from Turkomen Tabriz, but it seems likely they arrived in Western Anatolia directly from Timurid Central Asia sometime in the 1410s. They styled themselves 'Masters of Tabriz' and dominated the production of tilework in a sequence of important Ottoman buildings in Istanbul, Bursa and Edirne between 1420 and 1480 CE.

Henderson and Raby (1989) first established that the Master of Tabriz tile bodies were of the stonepaste type with the quartz particles bonded together with limited quantities of soda-lime frit. The composition of the single glaze analysed was approximately 3 wt% PbO, 14 wt% Na_2O, 1.5% wt% K_2O, 3.5 wt % CaO, and 3.5 wt% SnO_2, which is consistent with the use of soda-rich desert or coastal plant ashes. Simsek et al. (2019) confirmed, in their analysis of tiles from mosques in Edirne, that the Masters of Tabriz potters used stonepaste bodies containing some 75 wt% SiO_2, 12 wt% Al_2O_3, and 5 wt% Na_2O, but that, in this case, the glazes contain 20–30 wt% PbO and are free of tin. The glaze colorants used in the decoration of the Masters of Tabriz tiles were copper turquoise blue, manganese purple, and cobalt dark blue.

6.4 Miletus Ware

In contrast to the high-quality tiles produced in limited quantities by the Masters of Tabriz, the next major ceramic development in western Anatolia, was the introduction of Miletus Ware vessels which were mass-produced by Ottoman potters (Lane 1957b). Miletus Ware was named by Friedrich Sarre since he found it abundantly at Miletus, a site located on the Aegean coast of Anatolia, and assumed that it was locally manufactured (Sarre 1930–1931). Archaeological excavations have provided evidence of the production of Miletus Ware in four centres in Anatolia: Kütahya, Pergamon, Akçaalan, and Iznik which is considered as the major centre. Discoveries in Miletus itself suggest the local production of Miletus Ware, but this has yet to be confirmed.

The interior surfaces of Miletus Ware vessels feature painted decoration, usually in dark-blue, turquoise, purple and black colours, and the main motifs include flower rosettes or sunburst at the centre with radial lines around this central motif. The painted decoration is then covered with a transparent glaze. Our understanding of the production technology for Miletus ware is largely based on analysis by Burlot et al. (2020) of the glazes applied to the inner surfaces of 27 Miletus Ware sherds excavated from well-stratified contexts from five Turkish sites (Ephesus, Miletus, Pergamon, Sardis, and Iznik) as well as three sites located in the Crimea. The sherds span the period for the production of Miletus Ware from the mid-fifteenth century CE through to the end of the sixteenth century CE.

The bodies of Miletus ware are all clay-based, but in the majority of cases, a quartz-based slip similar in composition (82–92 wt% SiO_2, 3–9 wt% Al_2O_3, 2–4 wt% Na_2O, 0.5–3 wt% CaO) and microstructure to that of stonepaste bodies (Section 2.3) was applied over the clay body.

The glazes are all of the transparent lead-alkali type, but differ from earlier Islamic lead-alkali glazes in that their soda contents are significantly greater than their potash contents (6–33 wt% PbO, 5–17 wt% Na_2O, < 3 wt% K_2O), and that they also contain small amounts of boron and lithium. Similar to later Iznik wares, the most probable source of the alkali used in the production of Miletus ware glazes is a soda-rich evaporite from hot spring waters in western Turkey (Tite et al. 2016).

The underglaze decoration of Miletus Ware consists of four colours, turquoise (pale blue), purple, dark blue, and black. Copper oxide (>2.4 wt% CuO) is the colorant for the turquoise (pale blue) decoration, with the copper entirely present as Cu^{++} ions. Manganese-based minerals (>1.8 wt% MnO) provide the colorant for the purple decoration, but in this case, manganese-rich inclusions are present in the purple areas. Cobalt (0.4–2.0 wt% CoO) is the colorant for the blue decoration. These cobalt-rich areas contain higher copper and iron as well as some nickel, which results in the presence of inclusions of cobalt-iron and nickel-iron spinels (i.e., $CoFe_2O_4$ and $NiFe_2O_4$, respectively).

Finally, chromium (1.5 wt% Cr_2O_3) is the black colorant for the fine straight or curved lines of the decoration, the chromium colorant consisting of crushed, angular chromite particles which do not diffuse within the glaze. The black chromite particles are a chrome-rich spinel, composed mainly of Cr_2O_3, with subordinate Al_2O_3, MgO and Fe_2O_3 (>49 wt% Cr_2O_3 and approximately 16 wt% Al_2O_3, 13 wt% MgO, >4.5 wt% Fe_2O_3). In addition, some chromite particles contain relatively significant amounts of copper, manganese, cobalt and nickel, which again have probably diffused from the adjacent painted decorations in the glaze (Section 2.4.2). A possible source of the chromite pigment is the mines of magnesiochromite located in the provinces of Eskişehir, Bursa, Denizli, and Kütahya in western Anatolia.

Cobalt dark-blue, and chromium-based black pigments do not appear to have been used in the decoration of Byzantine and Beylik Wares from this region (Burlot et al. 2018).

6.5 Iznik Ware

Iznik ware, which was produced in Ottoman Turkey from the end of the fifteenth century CE onwards (Figure 11) (Henderson 1989; Tite 1989; Paynter et al. 2004). Initially produced as a substitute for imported Chinese blue-and-white porcelain, the generally accepted sequence for the development of Iznik pottery starts in about 1480 CE with 'Abraham of Kutahya' ware and continues through 'Golden Horn' wares by about 1530 CE, 'Damascus' wares by about 1540 CE, and Rhodos wares by about 1560 CE with its production continuing into the seventeenth century CE (Rogers and Ward 1988: 186–188). The decoration of the 'Abraham of Kutahya' and 'Golden Horn' wares is predominantly blue and white whereas that of the 'Damascus' and 'Rhodos' is polychrome

Because of the low iron contents and fine textures of the Iznik stonepaste bodies (about 1 wt% FeO) and slips (< 0.5 wt% FeO), together with the fact that they contain some 20 wt% of glassy frit, including a few percent of high lead frit, the result is an exceptionally hard, dense and glassy white body. The Iznik glaze is an essentially transparent lead-alkali glaze (20–40 wt% PbO, 8–14 wt% Na_2O) containing some 4–7 wt% SnO_2, of which the great majority is in solution. As in the case of Miletus ware (Section 6.4), the alkalis were obtained from Na-rich hot springs and wells in Western Turkey. As discussed by Paynter et al. (2004), the formulation of Iznik glazes makes them ideal for these high prestige ceramics. First, their high purity and in particular their very low iron oxide contents (typically < 0.5 wt% FeO) results in a completely colourless glaze of great clarity. Second, the high lead content results in a glaze with maximum gloss and brilliancy. The underglaze colorants used to decorate Iznik ware include cobalt blue, copper green and turquoise, manganese purple, chromite black, and finally, in the case of Rhodos ware, bole red (Tite 1989).

(a)   (b)

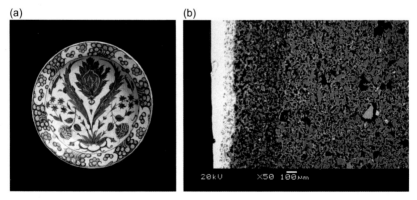

Figure 11 (a) An example of an Iznik ware (Ashmolean Museum, acc. no. EAX.3267), (b) a typical backscattered SEM photomicrograph of a section through transparent glaze into the slip and stonepaste body of an Iznik ware.

7 The Introduction of Islamic Ceramic Technology into Christian Europe

The introduction into Christian Europe of the technology for the production of glazed ceramics comparable to those produced in the Islamic world occurred via two routes. The first route was via al-Andalus (Section 7.1) and the second was via Ifriqiya (i.e., modern Tunisia) and Sicily (Section 7.2) (see also Figure 2). The subsequent developments in Christian Europe are discussed in Section 7.3.

7.1 The Beginning of Islamic Glazed Ceramic Production in al-Andalus

The first polychrome tin-opacified ceramics in al-Andalus, 'verde y manganeso', have been found in Cordoba (Madinat Qurtuba), dating to the Late Emirate period (888–912 CE) (Salinas and Pradell 2018). Subsequently, during the Umayyad Caliphate (929–1031 CE), when the new palace city was built in 939 CE at Madinat al-Zahra a few kilometres from Cordoba, production of 'verde y manganeso' increased dramatically. However, it still remained a luxury ceramic.

Salinas and Pradell (2020) have examined production debris associated with this period which was found in the pottery workshop quarter of Cordoba, as well as 'verde y manganeso' ceramics both from the palace site at Madinat al-Zahra and from domestic properties in Cordoba itself. Among the production debris was a fragment of a vessel containing a white glassy material. Analysis showed that this consisted of tin oxide and lead carbonate suggesting that the vessel was used in the production of a lead-tin calx, which with the addition of quartz and plant ash would have produced a tin glaze comparable in composition to that used in Abbasid Iraq (Matin et al. 2018).

The glazes of all the 'verde y manganeso' ceramics included both the high lead and lead-alkali types (30–60 wt% PbO and up to about 6 wt% $Na_2O + K_2O$). In contrast, the tin oxide contents of the palace ceramics were higher than those of the domestic ceramics from Cordoba (5–16 wt% as compared to 1–5 wt% SnO_2). Because of the high cost of tin oxide, this suggests that the palace ceramics were regarded as being of a higher quality than the domestic ceramics. The ceramics were decorated with copper-green (0.4–0.9 wt% CuO) and manganese-brown (1.8–4.4 wt% MnO), with a honey plain glaze (1.4–2.8 wt% FeO).

During both the Late Emirate Period and the Umayyad Caliphate, tin-opacified glazed ceramics were produced only in Cordoba, but were consumed all over the territory. Since, during the Umayyad Caliphate, present-day Portugal was part of al-Andalus, tin-opacified glazed ceramics found in Portugal were imported from

Cordoba. However, by the end of the Caliphate rule in early eleventh century CE, tin-opacified glazed ceramics were being produced in other parts of Spain, both Islamic and Christian.

In summary, tin opacified glazes were introduced into al-Andalus some hundred years before they appeared in Tunisia. On the basis of the composition of the lead-tin calx, the technology was most probably introduced from Abbasid Iraq at the time of urbanisation in al-Andalus in order to emulate the Abbasid court. In addition, it appears that two qualities of 'verde y manganeso' ceramics were being produced for different cliental at the same workshop in Cordoba.

7.2 Glazed Ceramic Production in Tunisia and Sicily

The production of polychrome glazed ware in Tunisia (*Ifriqiya*) during the ninth century, under Aghlabid rule, was probably its earliest production in the western Islamic lands. Schematic geometric, epigraphic and bird designs were painted in green and brown colours with a bright yellow background. The ware is known as 'Jaune de Raqqada' (Raqqada yellow), due to the large number of these wares found at the palace of Raqqada which was occupied from c.868–921 CE, initially under Aghlabid rule and from 909 CE, under Fatimid rule. This polychrome glazed ware was made by applying manganese-brown and copper-green pigments under an iron-yellow high lead transparent glaze (Ben Amara et al. 2001).

The second most representative early polychrome glaze production is called 'Sabra glazed ware' because a large number of these ceramics were found in the Fatimid capital of Sabra al-Mansuriyya which was founded in 947/948 CE and continued under the Zirid dynasty (972–1057 CE). Again, the wares were decorated by applying manganese-brown and copper-green pigments under an iron-yellow high lead transparent glaze.

Further groups of ceramics from Tunisia dating to the late tenth–early eleventh centuries CE and recovered from the sites of Bir Ftouha and Utica, located near to Carthage, have been subjected to detailed scientific examination (Salinas et al. 2020, 2022). Among the ceramics from Utica, a single glazed sherd is opacified and coloured yellow with lead antimonate particles, thus being the first documented yellow opaque lead antimonate glaze to be found in Tunisia (Salinas et al. 2022)

Following the Arab invasion of Sicily, the discovery of locally produced polychrome yellow glazed wares in Palermo, referred to as 'giallo di Palermo', which have clear similarities to the Tunisian polychrome glazed wares and are dated to the late ninth-early tenth centuries CE, provide direct evidence for an immediate transfer of ceramic technology (Sacco 2017; Ardizzone et al. 2018).

The subsequent development of Islamic ceramics in Sicily has also been investigated by Testolini (2018) who examined ceramics with opaque glazes from Castello San Pietro in Palermo and Pizzo Monaco on the northwest coast of Sicily dating from the ninth-tenth centuries CE through to the eleventh century CE. On the basis of petrographic examination in thin section, ceramics produced in Sicily can be distinguished from those produced in Tunisia and subsequently imported into Sicily.

Three groups of ceramics were identified with opaque glazes. The first group, dating to the tenth century CE, displayed manganese-brown, copper-green, and iron-amber decoration over an opaque white glaze which, since these glazes contained less than about 1% tin oxide, were probably opacified by the addition of crushed quartz. The second group, dating to around the mid-eleventh century CE, displayed manganese-brown, copper-green, iron-amber and opaque lead antimonate yellow decoration over a tin-opacified white glaze. The third group, also dating to the mid-eleventh century CE, displayed manganese-brown, opaque tin oxide white, and opaque lead antimonate yellow decoration over a copper-green glaze opacified with tin oxide. All the glazes were of the high lead type, but with the first group containing less lead and more alkali than the second and third groups (i.e., 40–50 wt% PbO plus about 3 wt% $Na_2O + K_2O$ compared to 50–60 wt% PbO plus about 1 wt% $Na_2O + K_2O$).

On the basis of the results of petrographic analysis, it was established that all three groups include both ceramics produced in Tunisia and subsequently imported into Sicily, and those produced in Sicily itself. However, of the ceramics examined, a higher proportion of the first group were produced in, rather than being imported into, Sicily (i.e., six produced in Sicily out of a total of seven) as compared to the second and third groups (i.e., for each group, only one produced in Sicily out of a total of three).

Hence, in addition to the single ceramic dating to early eleventh century CE, from Utica coloured and opacified with lead antimonate (as noted above), the results obtained by Testolini (2018) for these ceramics from Sicily further establishes that yellow lead antimonate and white tin oxide opacified glazed ceramics were being produced in both Tunisia and Sicily by the mid-eleventh century CE.

Therefore, tin-opacified white and lead antimonate opacified yellow glaze technologies spread into Tunisia, either directly or via Sicily, sometime in the eleventh century CE from Egypt, where they had been in use from the second half of the ninth century CE onwards (Section 4.1.1). Thus, contrary to what had originally been thought, there was a dynamic in which the opaque glaze tradition spread from Egypt to Tunisia and Sicily, and not from Tunisia to Egypt

7.3 Subsequent Developments in Christian Europe

Following the end of the rule of the Umayyad Caliphate in al-Andalus in the early eleventh century CE, Muslim control of the Iberian Peninsula progressively diminished with Toledo being lost in 1085 CE, Cordoba in 1236 CE, and Seville in 1248 CE, until only Granada, controlled by the Nasrid Dynasty (1232–1492 CE), remained (Guichard 2015)

The production of tin-opacified glazes outside Islamic territory is dated in the first half of the thirteenth century CE, in Catalonia (Barcelona) (Beltrán 2009; Di Febo et al. 2012; Peix et al. 2021), and in south-east of France (Marseille) (Marchesi et al. 1997), as well as in Northern Italy (Pisa, Orvieto) where it is referred to as Archaic maiolica (Whitehouse 1978). These tin-opacified glazed ceramics, typically with copper-green and manganese-black decoration, are extensively found in small quantities throughout northern Europe from the thirteenth century onwards, possibly as a result of being used as containers for commodities such as spices (Blake 2021). At a later date, from the mid fourteenth century CE onwards, Manises and Paterna in the province of Valencia became important centres for the production of Hispano-Moresque lusterware which was extensive exported northwards into the rest of Europe (Molera et al. 2001).

Although, during the second half of eleventh century CE, the Normans progressively increased their control of Sicily and parts of southern Italy (Wickham 2023), Muslim potters continued to operate in Sicily producing tin-opacified white and lead-antimonate-opacified yellow glazed ceramics up until 1233 CE. Thus, Muslim-inspired potters in Sicily and Apulia similarly began to produce tin-opacified glazed ceramics, known as Proto-maiolica in thirteenth century CE (Berti 1995).

Subsequently, during the Renaissance period, the range and quality of Italian maiolica progressively increased and by the end of the fifteenth century CE, a high level of artistic perfection had been achieved with the introduction of *istoriato* plates and vessels which were decorated with narrative and historical scenes (Tite 2009). Additionally, Medici porcelain, the first European porcelain with well-documented surviving pieces, was produced in Florence from around 1575 CE until the death of the Grand Duke Francesco in 1587, the inspiration for its production being the import of both Chinese blue-and-white porcelain and Islamic blue-and-white Iznik ware (Tite 1991). Eventually, tin-opacified glazed pottery spread to France, the Netherlands, Germany, and England, which was variously known as faience, fayence, and delftware.

8 Conclusions

The development and production of Islamic ceramics are closely intertwined with the social and economic dynamics of their respective periods. The extent to which these influences can be traced depends on various factors, including the quality of published archaeological data, and the accessibility and condition of excavated materials suitable for scientific analysis (i.e., not weathered). Despite advancements, the scale and organization of pottery workshops remain largely unknown. The establishment of new capitals and the growth of large and urban centres such as Baghdad, Samarra, Fustat, and Samarqand created favourable conditions and increased demands for innovative ceramic creations, often involving the migration of skilled craftspeople from various regions. However, there are exceptions to this narrative. Kashan, for instance, was a relatively small town at the time, impacted by the Mongol invasion after decades of production, yet it persisted in producing some of the most exquisite ceramics in the history of the Islamic World.

Pottery workshops and kiln evidence are frequently mentioned in reports (see, e.g., Nishapur (Wilkinson 1973: 259), Samarqand (Shishkina and Pavchinskaja 1999), Isfahan (Rugiadi (2011, 2010), and Moshkin Tepe (Sedighian 2010; Matin 2022), yet there is a notable absence of comprehensive publications on major kiln sites throughout the Islamic World. We know from archaeological excavations as well as some written sources that there were large industrial zones attached to cities such as in Raqqa and Fustat. In other cases, there seems that there were smaller-scale villages or workshops specialising in pottery production. Evidence of kiln rods has been discovered as early as the ninth century in the production of glazed ceramics from Basra. The spread and continuity of this kiln technology are evidenced by findings of kiln rods across the Islamic World, including Samarqand, Nishapur, Takht-i Suleiman, Kashan, Moshkin Tepe, Balis-Meskene, and Pechina (al-Andalus) (see Thiriot 1997). It appears that vertical updraught kilns were commonly used, with the fire chamber positioned at the bottom and heat directed upwards. Rods were inserted into the circular kiln walls at regular intervals, forming shelves upon which vessels were placed. Open bowls were positioned inside clay saggars to protect them during firing. Clay tripods may or may not have been used to separate the bowls from each other or from the saggars. This stacking method involved placing several bowls on top of each other and positioning them on kiln rods, either upright or upside down, distinguishable by the direction of glaze runs (Figures 12a and b). It is regrettable that we possess limited knowledge about kiln technologies themselves, as they could offer significant insights into potential connections and innovations across the region.

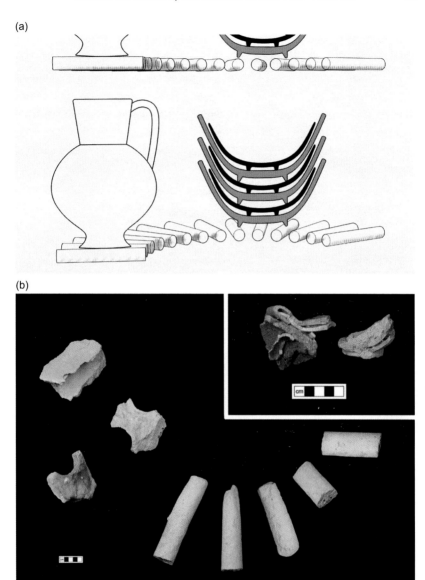

Figure 12 (a) Schematic photo illustrating an example of arrangement of vessels on rod shelves in an Islamic kiln. The open bowls were placed inside clay saggars. (b) examples of kiln rods, and fragments of kiln walls showing the holes where the rods were inserted, as well as wasters showing the bowls (stonepaste) placed into clay saggars.

However, it is in the study of Islamic ceramics themselves that several aspects of the social and cultural history, such as dynamics of economy, trade patterns, and movements of craftspeople, can be traced. The intricate technological complexities of these developments leave little doubt that they must have been transferred alongside the craftspeople who possessed the knowledge of these technologies. The scientific analysis of Islamic ceramics conducted thus far has revealed significant waves of technological innovation and transfer. While by no means exhaustive, these findings shed light on some of the social and cultural changes of the period. One aspect of Islamic pottery that seems to have sparked ceramic innovations over the long term is the significance of colour. The quest to achieve a white surface, inspired by imported Chinese ceramics, led to the development of two technologies: white tin opacification and stonepaste bodies. In addition, the use of new mineral pigments to achieve different colours in the glaze required extensive experimentation and practice, which may not be immediately apparent without considering the technological aspects of their production.

The earliest innovations in the development of Islamic glazed ceramics took place in the Umayyad period towards the end of the eighth century in the Eastern Mediterranean. This phase saw the development of regional fine pottery, as well as the first use of lead stannate yellow, often combined with copper green and/or manganese brown, and later tin oxide white in ceramic glazes of the CGW and YGF wares. This technological innovation brought a radically new colour palette to glazed ceramics that did not exist before.

The relocation of the capital from Damascus in Syria to Baghdad in Iraq in 762 CE, following the Abbasid overthrow of the Umayyad dynasty, appears to have encouraged the movement of craftspeople to the southern Mesopotamia region. The Abbasid patronage of major cities in Iraq such as Baghdad and Samarra, as well as expansive trade with Tang China, brought new dynamics to Islamic industry, particularly ceramics. The burgeoning economy of the Abbasids created a demand for potters to introduce innovative technological advancements. The technology of tin-based opacification of ceramics, which had been practiced before in the CGW and YGF wares of Egypt and the Levant, further developed into radically new, fine, luxury wares of the so-called Samarra-type pottery. This pottery featured not just the use of white tin-opacified glazes, but a wide range of styles provided by other new complex technological innovations such as lustre and cobalt blue decoration.

Following the decline of Iraq in the tenth century CE and the relocation of the Fatimid capital from Tunisia to Egypt in 969 CE, there seems to have been an influx of potters from Iraq to Egypt. This shift, compounded by Egypt's growing economic prominence under the Fatimids, facilitated the dissemination of lustre technology from Iraq to Egypt. Chemical analysis of Egyptian pottery show that potters adopted to local materials. In Egypt, potters used local Nile Alluvium clay to produce ceramic bodies. It also appears that the white tin-opacified glazes have lead/tin ratios different than those of Samarra-type pottery which conveys the use of distinct calx recipes in Egypt.

In addition, it is during this period that stonepaste bodies appear to be developed in Egypt, featuring another significant technological invention of the Islamic period. After the year 1171 CE, Egypt experienced significant political changes when the Ayyubids took over Egypt. It appears though that Egypt remained a prominent centre of political, cultural, and economic activity in the region. In the case of stonepaste body technology, there is limited evidence to trace its movement across Egypt, Syria, and Iran. However, the different recipes identified through chemical analyses once again highlight how potters adjusted their techniques based on the materials that were readily available or better suited to their new locations.

This adaptability is also evident in the production of more local inventions such as the Eastern Iranian slip-painted pottery of the tenth century. Chemical analyses demonstrate various recipes for the white slip, using quartz, high-aluminium clay, or dehydrated pyrophyllite, as it continued to be produced in different sites across the Central Asian region.

During latter part of the fourteenth century, Timur's forceful relocation of skilled craftsmen to key Timurid cities, notably Samarqand, and his significant artistic patronage contributed to thriving crafts and construction, ceramics included. The underglaze technique further developed, and the subsequent westward migration from Samarqand fostered another wave of the potters' movement and knowledge transfer, leading to further developments in pottery and tile production in Anatolia (i.e., modern Turkey).

The movement of craftspeople across vast distances, spanning thousands of kilometres, was a pivotal aspect of Islamic history. They traversed diverse landscapes, from mountains to deserts, relying on various modes of transportation. Evidence from osteological findings, textual records, and manuscript illuminations highlights the importance of pack animals such as donkeys, which were crucial for local transport, as well as camels, known for their endurance, carrying capacity, and cost-effectiveness. Additionally, waterways played a significant role in transportation, especially for long-distance trade. It was long-term maritime transportation that contributed to the emergence of globally oriented economic systems. Seasonal maritime trade routes, such as those across the Indian Ocean, were crucial for connecting different regions. Nevertheless, some faced challenges like ship damage and plundering along the way.

Stylistic studies of Islamic pottery have already established how different motifs and styles were borrowed from various materials such as textiles, metalwork, and manuscripts. However, the technological examination of ceramics sheds light on aspects of cross-technological interactions, such as the interconnectedness between ceramic production and pigment mining. One extensively studied example is the cobalt mine of Kashan, where cobalt pigment was initially used in Kashan pottery but later became the primary source of cobalt used across the Islamic World and even in China during the Yuan and early Ming dynasties. Another innovation was the use of chromite black, first observed in Eastern Iranian slip-painted pottery before becoming prevalent in underglaze-painted wares throughout the Islamic World. The strategic location of significant chromite mines in eastern Iran, along with references to these mines in Abu'l Qasim Kashani's manuscript as a source of chromite in under-glaze painted wares, suggests their importance and continuity throughout the Islamic period. Moreover, similar to the cobalt mine, the proximity of these mining sites to Eastern Iranian pottery workshops may have contributed to their integration into ceramic technology in the tenth century CE.

References

Aarab, A., Shojaee-Esfahani, A., Xu, S., and Yang, Y., 2025. Characterizing the earliest black and turquoise wares in 12th century Persia. *Journal of Archaeological Sciences*: *Reports*, 61, paper 104928 (11pgs).

Akbari, A., 2019. *Shaah-kureh*, Kashan: Moassesseh-i Kashan, Khaneh-i Sufal [in Persian].

Al-Hassan, 2009. An eighth century Arabic Treatise on the colouring of glass Kitāb al-Durra al-Maknūna (The Book of the Hidden Pearl) of Jābir Ibn Ḥayyān (c.721_c. 815), *Arabic Sciences and Philosophy*, 19(01), 1–36.

Allan, J. W., 1973. Abū'l-Qāsim's Treatise on Ceramics, *IRAN*, 11, 111–120.

Ardizzone, F., Pezzini, E., and Sacco, V., 2018. Chapter 18 Aghlabid Palermo: Written sources and archaeological evidence, in G. D. Anderson, C. Fenwick, and M. Rosser-Owen (eds.), *The Aghlabids and Their Neighbors: Art and Material Culture in Ninth-Century North Africa*. Boston: Brill, 362–381.

Armstrong, P., Hatcher, H., and Tite, M., 1997. Changes in Byzantine glazing technology from the ninth to thirteenth centuries, in Gabrielle Demians d'archimbaud (ed.), *La céramique médiévale en Méditerranée, Actes du 6e Congrès*, Aix-en-Provence. Narration, Aix-en-Provence. 6, 225–229.

Bagci, Y., 2016. Colours of the Caliphs, Shades of the Thughur al Sham: Revisiting Early Islamic Ceramics from 1935–1948 Gozlukule Excavations in Tarsus (Southern Turkey), unpublished PhD thesis, Leiden: University of Leiden.

Bahgat, A. B., and Massoul, F., 1930. *La Céramique Musulmane de l'Egypte*, Cairo.

Ben Amara, A., Schvoerer, M., Daoulatli, A., and Rammah, M., 2001. 'Jaune de Raqqada' et autres couleurs de céramiques glaçurées aghlabides de Tunisie (IX – X siècles), *Revue d'Archéométrie*. Imprimerie de l'Institut français d'archéologie orientale. 25, 179–186.

Bazl, F., 1939. The ceramic arts (D): Contemporary techniques, in A. U. Pope and Ph. Ackerman (eds.), *A Survey of Persian Art*, vol. IV, London: Oxford University Press, 1703–1706.

Beltrán, J., 2009. Pisa arcaica decorada en verde y/o manganeso de Barcelona y cerámica vidriada: Un contexto de la primera mitad del siglo XIII, *Actas del VIII Congreso Internacional de Cerámica Medieval en el Mediterráneo*, 2, 635–651.

Ben Amara, A., Schvoerer, M., Thierrin-Michael, G., and Rammah, M., 2005. Distinction de céramiques glaçurées aghlabides ou fatimides (IXe- XIe siècles, Ifriqiya) par la mise en évidence de diférences de texture au niveau de l'interface glaçure – terre cuite, *Archéo-Sciences*, 29, 35–42.

Berti, G., 1995. Introduzione di nuove tecniche ceramiche nell'Italia centro-settentrionale, in E. Boldrini, and R. Francovich (eds.), *Acculturazione e mutamenti: Prospettive nell'archeologia medieval del Mediterraneo*. Firenze: All'Insegna del Giglio, 263–283.

Blake, H., 2021. Archaic Maiolicas in the North, c. 1280–1450, in J. V. G. Mallet and E. P. Sani (eds.), *Papers of a Symposium Held at Oxford in Celebration of Timothy Wilson's Catalogue of Maiolica in the Ashmolean Museum*. Oxford: Ashmolean Museum, 25–56.

Bongianino, U. V., 2014. 'And their figures and colours should be different' incised and carved glazed wares from Fustat (9th–12th century) in the Martin Collection (International Museum of Ceramics in Faenza) – part I, *Faenza*, 2, 28–48.

Bongianino, U. V., 2015. 'And their figures and colours should be different' incised and carved glazed wares from Fustat (9th–12th century) in the Martin Collection (International Museum of Ceramics in Faenza) – part II, *Faenza*, 2, 8–31.

Bongianino, U. V., 2017. 'And their figures and colours should be different' incised and carved glazed wares from Fustat (9th–12th century) in the Martin Collection (International Museum of Ceramics in Faenza) – part III, *Faenza*, 1, 9–25.

Boucharlat, R., 1993. Pottery in Susa during the Seleucid, Parthian and early Sasanian Periods, in U. Finkbeiner (ed.), *Materialien zur Archäologie der Seleukiden – und Partherzeit im südlichen Babylonien und im Golfgebiet*, Tübingen: Deutches Archäologisches Institute Abteilung Baghdad, 42–57.

Bouquillon, A., Coquinot, Y., and Doublet, C., 2012. Chapter III: Pottery study and analyses, in R. Rante and A. Collinet (eds.), *Nishapur Revisited: Stratigraphy and Ceramics of the Qohandez*. Oxford: Oxbow Books, 56–135.

Brughmans, T., and Poblome, J., 2016. Roman bazaar or market economy? Explaining tableware distributions through computational modelling, *Antiquity*, 90(350), 293–408.

Burlot, J., Waksman, S. Y., Böhlendorf-Arslan, B. et al., 2018. The early Turkish Pottery productions in Western Anatolia: Provenances, contextualization and techniques, in F. Yenişehirlioğlu (ed.), *Proceedings of the 11th International Congress AIECM3 on Medieval and Modern Period*

Mediterranean Ceramics, Antalya, 19–24 October 2015. Ankara: Koç University VEKAM, 427–430.

Burlot, J., Waksman, S. Y., Bellot-Gurlet, L., and Simsek-Franci, G., 2020. The glaze production technology of an early Ottoman pottery (mid-14th–16th century): The case of 'miletus ware', *Journal of Archaeological Science: Reports*, 29, 1–11.

Burlot, J., and Waksman, S. Y., 2021. Cultural, technological, and economic changes in Western Anatolia: Observing the Byzantine-Ottoman transition (13th–15th Centuries) through Glazed Tableware, in N. D. Kontogiannis, B. Böhlendorf-Arslan, and F. Yenişehirlioğlu (eds.), *Glazed Wares as Cultural Agents in the Byzantine, Seljuk, and Ottoman Lands*. Istanbul: Koç University Press, 157–190.

Centlivres-Demont, M., 1971. *Une communauté de potiers en Iran: le centre de Meybod (Yazd)*, Wiesbaden: L. Reichert in Kommision bei O. Harrassowitz.

Cheng, M., 2016. Persian glazed ceramics: Evidence of early maritime Silk Road, *Public Archaeology*, 9, 5865.

Clark, R., Cridland, L., Kariuki, B., Harris, K., and Withnall, R., 1995. Synthesis, structural characterisation and Raman spectroscopy of the inorganics pigments lead tin yellow types I and II and lead antimony yellow: Their identification on medieval paintings and manuscripts, *Journal of the Chemical Society, Dalton Transactions*, 16, 2577–2582.

Degryse, P., Gonzalez, S. N., Vanhaecke, F., Dillis, S., and Van Ham-Meert, 2024. The rise and fall of antimony: Sourcing the 'colourless' in Roman glass, *Journal of Archaeological Science: Reports*, 53, 104344, 1–8.

Di Febo, R., Fernández, M. M., Capelli, C. et al., 2012. Noves dades sobre la producció de ceràmica medieval de Barcelona. La caracterització arqueomètrica del taller del Carrer de Carders, Quaderns D'Arqueologia I Historia de La Ciutat De Barcelona (Quarhis), Epoca II, Numero 08, 150–164. Barcelona: Museu D'Historia De Barcelona.

Fiorentino, S., 2021. A Tale of two legacies: Byzantine and Egyptian influences in the manufacture and supply of glass Tessarea under the Umayyad Caliphate (661–750 AD), *Heritage*, 4, 2810–2834.

Franchi, R., Tonghini, C., Paloschi, F., and Soldi, M., 1995. Medieval Syrian Fritware: Materials and manufacturing techniques, in P. Vincenzini (ed.), *The Ceramics Cultural Heritage*, TECHNA- Monographs in Materials and Society 2, Faenza: Techna, 197–205.

Freestone, I.C., Yeğingil, Z., and Arık, R., 2009. Scientific analysis of glazed tile from the Seljuq Palace of Kubad-Âbâd, Lake Beyşehir, Turkey, in B. McCarthy, E. Salzman Chase, L. Allison Cort, J. G. Douglas, and P. Jett (eds.), *Scientific Research on Historic Asian Ceramics: Proceedings of the*

Fourth Forbes Symposium at the Freer Gallery of Art, Washington, DC: Archetype Publications, 3–8.

Frierman, J. D., 1970. Physical and chemical properties of some medieval near eastern glazed, in R. Berger (ed.), *Scientific Methods in Medieval Archeology*. Berkeley: University of California Press, 379–388.

Frye, R., 1975. The SĀMĀNIDS, in R. Frye (ed.), *The Cambridge History of Iran*, Cambridge: Cambridge University Press, 136–161.

Gayraud, R.P., Vallauri, L., 2017. *Fouilles d'Isṭabl 'Antar : Céramiques d'ensembles des IXe et Xe siècles*, Le Caire: Institut français d'archéologie orientale du Caire.

Gill, M. S., Rehren, Th., and Freestone, I., 2014. Tradition and indigeneity in Mughal architectural glazed tiles, *Journal of Archaeological Science*, 49, 546–555.

Gill, M. S., and Rehren, Th., 2017. An analytical evaluation of historic glazed tiles from Makli and Lahore, Pakistan, *Journal of Archaeological Science: Reports*, 16, 266–275.

Golombek, L., Mason, R., and Proctor, P., 2014. *Persian Pottery in the First Global Age: The Sixteenth and Seventeenth Centuries*, Leiden, Netherlands: Brill.

Grabar, O., Holod, R., Knustad, J., and Trousdale, W., 1978. *City in the Desert: Qasr al-Hayr East*, 2 vols, Cambridge, MA: Harvard University Press.

Guichard, P., 2015. *Esplendor y fragilidad de al-Andalus*, Granada: Fundación El Legado andalusí.

Guillermina, J., Peli, A., and Makariou, S., 2005. *Suse: terres cuites islamiques*, Gand: Snoeck, Paris: Musée du Louvre.

Gulmini, M., Giannini, R., Lega, A. M., Manna, G., and Mirti, P., 2013. Technology of production of Ghaznavid Glazed Pottery from Bust and Lashkar-i Bazar (Afghanistan), *Archaeometry*, 55(4), 569–590.

Guy, J., 2005. Early ninth-century Chinese export ceramics and the Persian Gulf connection: The Belitung shipwreck evidence, in Éditions Findakly (ed.), *Chine-Méditerranée, Routes et échanges de la céramique jusqu'au XVIe Siècle*, TAOCI, Paris: Musée Guimet, vol. 4, 9–20.

Hallett, J., 2000. Trade and Innovation: The Rise of the Pottery Industry in Abbasid Basra, unpublished DPhil thesis, Trinity College, University of Oxford.

Hamed, I., 1988. *Introduction à l'étude archéologique des deux routes syrienne et égyptienne de pélerinage au nord-ouest de l'Arabie Saoudite*, unpublished PhD thesis, Université de Provence.

Hill, D. V., 2006. *The Materials and Technology of Glazed Ceramics from the Deh Luran Plain, Southwestern Iran: A Study in Innovation*, BAR International Series.

Harvey, E., 2021. The decline of Green-Glazed Jars after the early Abbasid Period, *Islamic Law and Society*. Oxford: John and Erica Hedges, 28, 415–457.

Henderson, J., 1989. *Iznik Ceramics: A Technical Examination, in Iznik– the Pottery of Ottoman Turkey* (eds. N. Atasoy and J. Raby), 65–69, 84–87, London: Alexandria Press.

Henderson. J., and Raby J., 1989. The technology of sixteenth-century Turkish tiles: An interim statement on the origins of the Iznik industry, *World Archaeology*, 21, 115–132.

Henshaw, C. M., 2010. *Early Islamic Ceramics and Glazes of Akhsiket, Uzbekistan*, Unpublished PhD dissertation, Department of Archaeology, University of College London.

Holakooei, P., de Laprouse, J. F., Car., F. et al., 2019. Non-invasive scientific studies on the provenance and technology of early Islamic ceramics from Afrasiyab and Nishapur, *Journal of Archaeological Science: Reports*, 24, 759–772.

Holakooei, P., Mishmastnehi, M., Moloodi Arani, A., Röhrs, S., and Franke, U., 2023. Materials and technique of lajvardina ceramics from the thirteenth to fourteenth century Iran, *Archaeological and Anthropological Studies*, 15(33), 1–15.

Hourani,G. F., 1995. *Arab Seafaring in the Indian Ocean in Ancient and Early Medieval Times*, Revised and expanded by John Carswel, Princeton: Princeton University Press.

Hurst, D., and Freestone, I., 1996. Lead glazing technique from a medieval kiln site at Hanley Swan, Worcestershire, *Medieval Ceramics*, 20, 13–18.

Jenkins-Madina, M., 2006. *Raqqa Revisited: Ceramics of Ayyubid Syria*, New York: Metropolitan Museum of Art.

Kennet, D., 2004. *Sasanian and Islamic Pottery from Ras al-Khaimah: Classification Chronology and Analysis of Trade in the Western Indian Ocean*, British Archaeological Reports International Series 1248/Society for Arabian Studies Monographs 1, Oxford: Archaeopress.

Kervran, M., 1977. Les niveaux islamiques du secteur oriental de l'Apadana, II. – Le matériel céramique, *Cahiers de la Délégation Archéologique Française en Iran*, 7, 75–161.

Kevran, M., 1979. Une sucrerie d'époque islamique sur la rive droite du chaour à Suse: II, le material archaeologique, *Cahiers de la Délégation Archéologique Française en Iran*, 10, 177–237.

Kiefer, Ch., 1956. Les Céramiques siliceuses d'Anatolie et du Moyen Orient, *Bulletin de la Société française de Céramique*, 30, 3–24.

Kingery, W. D., and Vandiver, P. B., 1986. *Ceramic Masterpieces: Art, Structure and Technology*, New York: The Free Press, 135–147.

Klesner, C. E., MacDonald, B. L., Dussubieux L., Akymbek, Y., and Vandiver, P. B., 2019. Local production and long-distance trade of Islamic glazed ceramics in Central Asia: a compositional analysis of ceramics from Southern Kazakhstan by NAA and LA-ICP-MS, *Journal of Archaeological Science: Reports*, 26, 101905.

Klesner, C., Renson, V., Akymbek, Y., and Killick, D., 2021. Investigation of provenances of Early Islamic lead glazes from northern Central Asia using elemental and lead isotope analyses, *Archaeological and Anthropological Sciences*, 13(203), 1–36.

Koss, K., McCarthy, B., Chase, E. S., and Smith, D., 2009. Analysis of Persian Painted Minai Ware, in B. McCarthy, E. S. Chase, L. A. Cort, J. G. Douglas, and P. Jett (eds.), *Scientific Research on Historic Asian Ceramics: Proceedings of Fourth Forbes Symposium at the Freer Gallery of Art*, London: Archetype Publications, 33–47.

Krahl, R. (ed.), 2001. *Shipwrecked: Tang Treasures and Monsoon Winds*, Exhibition Catalogue, Washington, DC: Smithsonian Institution, Singapore: National Heritage Board.

Kühn, H., 1968. Lead-tin yellow, *Studies in Conservation*, 13, 1, 7–33.

Lane, A., 1947. *Early Islamic Pottery: Mesopotamia, Egypt, and Persia*, London: Faber & Faber.

Lane, A., 1957a. *Later Islamic Pottery: Persia, Syria, Egypt, Turkey*, London: Faber & Faber.

Lane, A., 1957b. The Ottoman Pottery of Isnik, *Ars Orientalis*, 2, 247–81.

Logar, N., 1995. Die Keramik des mittelalterlichen Wohnkomplexes in Resafa, *Damaszener Mitteilumgen*, 8, 269–291.

Marchesi, H., Thiriot, J., and Vallauri, L., 1997. *Marseille, les ateliers de potiers du XIIIe s. et le quartier Sainte-Barbe (Ve-XVIIIe s.)*, Paris: Editions de la Maison des Sciences de l'Homme.

Martínez Ferreras, V., Fusaro, A., Gurt Esparraguera, J. M., et al., 2019. The Islamic Ancient Termez through the lens of ceramics: A new archaeological and archaeometric study, *IRAN*, 58(2),1–29.

Mason, R. B., 1991. Petrography of Islamic ceramics. in A. Middleton and I. C. Freestone (eds.), *Recent Developments in Ceramic Petrology*, London: British Museum Occasional Paper no. 81, 185–209.

Mason, R. B., 1994. *Islamic Glazed Pottery: 700–1250*, Unpublished DPhil dissertation, University of Oxford.

Mason, R. B., 1996. The response I: Petrography and provenance of Timurid ceramics, in L. Golombek, R. B. Mason, and G. A. Bailey (eds.), *Tamerlane's Tableware: A New Approach to the Chinoiserie Ceramics of Fifteenth- and Sixteenth-Century Iran*, Costa Meza, Toronto: Mazda Publishers in association with the Royal Ontario Museum, 16–56.

Mason, R. B., 2004. S*hine Like the Sun: lustre-Painted and Associated Pottery from the Medieval Middle East*, Costa Mesa: Mazda Publishers in association with Royal Ontario Museum.

Mason, R. B., and Keall, J., 1990. Petrography of Islamic Pottery from Fustat, *Journal of the American Research Centre in Egypt*, 27, 165–184.

Mason, R. B., and Tite, M. S., 1994. The beginnings of Islamic stonepaste technology, *Archaeometry*, 36(1), 77–91.

Mason, R. B., and Tite, M. S., 1997. The beginnings of the tin-opacification of pottery glazes, *Archaeometry*, 39, 41–58.

Mason, R. B., Tite, M. S., Paynter, S., and Salter, C., 2001. Advances in polychrome ceramics in the Islamic World of the 12th century AD, *Archaeometry*, 43(2), 191–209.

Masuya, T., 1997. *The Ilkhanid Phase of Takht-i Sulaiman*, Unpublished PhD dissertation, New York University.

Matin, M., 2016. *Revisiting the origins of Islamic glazed pottery: A technological examination of 8th–10th century AD ceramics from Islamic lands*, University of Oxford, Unpublished DPhil thesis.

Matin, M., 2019. Tin-based opacifiers in archaeological glass and ceramic glazes: A review and new perspectives, *Archaeological and Anthropological Sciences*, 11(4), 1155–1167.

Matin, M., 2020. The technology of medieval Islamic ceramics: A study of two persian manuscripts, in O. Watson (ed.), *Ceramics of Iran: Islamic Pottery in the Sarikhani Collection*, New Haven: Yale University Press, 459–487.

Matin, M., 2022. A medieval stonepaste ceramic production site in Moshkin Tepe, Iran: ceramics, wasters, and manufacturing equipment, *IRAN*, 62(2), 1–15.

Matin, M., and Matin, M., 2012. Egyptian fainece glazing by the cementation method part 1: An investigation of the glazing powder composition and glazing mechanism, *Journal of Archaeological Science*, 39(3), 763–776.

Matin, M., and Ownby, M., 2023. Early stonepaste ceramic technology in Fustat, Egypt, *Journal of Archaeological Science: Reports*, 104105, 1–9.

Matin, M., and Pollard, M., 2015. Historical accounts of Cobalt Ore processing from the Kashan Mine, Iran, *IRAN*, v.53/1, 171–183.

Matin, M., and Pollard, M., 2017. From ore to pigment: A description of the minerals and an experimental study of Cobalt ore processing from the Kāshān mine, Iran, *Archaeometry*, 59(4), 731–46.

Matin, M., Tite, M., and Watson, O., 2018. On the origins of tin-opacified ceramics glazes: new evidence from early Islamic Egypt, the Levant, Mesopotamia, Iran, and Central Asia, *Journal of Archaeological Sciences*, 97, 42–66.

McCarthy, B. E., 1996. *Microstructural and compositional studies of the technology and durability of ceramic glazes from Nippur, Iraq, ca. 250BC – 1450 AD*, unpublished PhD thesis, Baltimore: John Hopkins University.

McClary, R. P., 2016. A new approach to *mina'i* wares: Chronology and decoration, *Persica*, 25, 1–20.

McClary, R. P., 2022. Rare and Complex Wares: A study of vessels and sherds decorated with both Mina'i and Lustre techniques, *Journal of Material Cultures in the Museum World*, 3, 235–266.

Mishmastnehi, M., 2018. *Technical and Archaeological Studies of Persian Windmills and their Millstones in Eastern Iran*, Unpublished PhD dissertation, Freie Universität Berlin.

Molera, J., Pradell, T., Salvadó, N., and Vendrell-Saz, M., 1999, Evidence of tin oxide recrystallization in opacified lead glazes, *Journal of American Ceramic Society*, 82(10), 2871–2875.

Molera, J., Mesquida, M., Pérez-Arantegui, J., Pradell, T., and Vendrell, M., 2001. Luster recipes from medieval workshop in Paterna, *Archaeometry*, 43(4), 455–460.

Molera, J., Bayes, C., Roura, P., Crespo, D., and Pradell, T., 2007. Key Parameters in the Production of Mesieval Lustre Colors and Shines, *Journal of American Ceramic Society*, 90(7), 2245–2254.

Molera, J., Martínez Ferreras, V., Fusaro, A. et al., 2020. Islamic glazed ware from ancient Termez (southern Uzbekistan): Raw materials and techniques, *Journal of Archaeological Science: Reports*, 102169, 1–11.

Morgan, P., and Leatherby, J., 1971. Excavated ceramics from Sirjan, in J. Allan and C. Roberts (eds.), *Syria and Iran: Three Studies in Medieval Ceramics*, Oxford: Oxford University Press, 23–173.

Moroni, B., and Conti, C., 2006. Technological features of Renaissance pottery from Deruta (Umbria, Italy): An experimental study, *Applied Clay Science*, 33, 230–246.

Nassir Khusraw, 2001. *Book of Travels*, edited and translated by W. S. Thackston, Costa Mesa.

Norris, D., and Watson, O., 2021. Illuminating the imperceptible, researching *Mina'i* ceramics with digital imaging techniques, *Journal of Imaging*, 7(11), 233, 1–11.

Northedge, A., Bamber, A., and Roaf, M., 1988. *Excavations at 'Āna: Qal'a Island*, Warminster: British School of Archaeology in Iraq and the Directorate of Antiquities by Aris & Philips.

Northedge, A., Kennet, D., 1994. The Samarra Horizon, in E. Grube (ed.), *Cobalt and Lustre, The Nasser D. Khalili Collection of Islamic Art*, V IX, Oxford: Khalili Research Centre, University of Oxford, 21–35.

O'Kane, B., 2011. Tiles of many Hues: The development or Iranian Cuerda Seca tiles and the transfer of tilework technology, in J. M. Bloom and S. S. Blair (eds.), *And Diverse Are Their Hues: Color in Islamic Art and Culture*. London: Yale University Press, 177–203.

Osete-Cortina, L., Doménech-Carbó, M. T., Doménech, A., Yusá-Marco, D. J., and Ahmadi, H., 2010. Multimethod analysis of Iranian Ilkhanate ceramics from the Takht-e Soleyman Palace, *Analytical and Bioanalytical Chemistry*, 397, 319–29.

Öztürk, Ç., Şimşek-Franci, G., and Kuşoğlu, İ. M., 2022. An archaeometric assessment study of Seljuk period glazed tiles from Kılıçarslan Square (Konya, Turkey), *Heritage Science*, 10, 174, 1–16.

Pace, M., Bianco Prevot, A., Mirti, P., and Venco Ricciardi, R., 2008. The technology of production of Sasanian glazed pottery from Veh Ardasir (Central Iraq), *Archaeometry*, 50(4), 591–605.

Paynter, S.C., 2001. *The development of vitreous materials in the ancient Near East and Egypt*, Unpublished DPhil thesis, University of Oxford.

Paynter, S., 2008. Links between glazes and glass in mid-2nd millennium BC Mesopotamia and Egypt, in A. J. Shortland, Th. Rehren, and I. C. Freestone (eds.), *From Mine to Microscope*, Oxford: Oxbow Books, 93–108.

Paynter, S., Okyar, F., Wolf, S., and Tite, M. S., 2004. The production technology of Iznik pottery – a reassessment, *Archaeometry*, 46, 421–437.

Peix, J., Fernández, M. M., and Garrigós, J. B., 2021. The case of black and green tin glazed pottery from Barcelona between 13th and 14th century: Analysing its production and its decorations, *Journal of Archaeological Science: Reports*, 38(3), 1–16.

Philon, H., 1980. *Early Islamic Ceramics*, Athens: Benaki Museum.

Porter, V., and Watson, O., 1987. 'Tell Minis' wares, in J. Allan and C. Roberts (eds.), *Syria and Iran: Three Studies in Medieval Ceramics*, Oxford: Published by Oxford University Press for the Board of the Faculty of Oriental Studies, University of Oxford, 175–248.

Poulsen, V., 1957. Les poteries médiévales, in P. J. Rus, V. Poulsen, and E., Hammershaimb (eds.), *Hama: Fouilles et recherches de la Fondation Carlsberg 1931–1938, IV/2*, Copenhagen: Nationalmuseet, 115–283.

Pradell, T., 2016. Lustre and nanostructure- ancient technologies revisited, in P. Dillman, L. Bellot-Gurlet, and I. Nenner (eds.), *Nanoscience and Cultural Heritage*, Paris: Atlantis Press, 3–39.

Pradell, T., Molera, J., Smith, A. D., and Tite, M. S., 2008. Early Islamic lustre from Egypt, Syria and Iran (10th to 13th century AD). *Journal of Archaeological Science*, 35, 2649–2662.

Priestman, S. M. N., 2005. Settlement and Ceramics in Southern Iran: An Analysis of the Sasanian and Islamic Periods in the Williamson Collection, Durham: Unpublished MA thesis, Department of Archaeology, Durham University.

Priestman, S. M. N., 2011. Opaque Glazed Wares: The definition, dating and distribution of a key Iraqi ceramic export in the Abbasid period, *Iran*, 49, 89–113.

Priestman, S. M. N., 2016. The Silk Road or the Sea? Sasanian and Islamic Exports to Japan, *Journal of Islamic Archaeology*, 3(1), 1–35.

Priestman, S. M. N., 2021. *Ceramic Exchange and the Indian Ocean Economy (AD 400–1275)*, Volume I: Analysis, London: The British Museum.

Rawson, J., Tite, M. S., and Hughes, M. J., 1988. The export of Tang Sancai wares: Some recent research, *Transaction of the Oriental Ceramic Society*, 52, 39–62.

Redford, S., 1995. Medieval ceramics from Samsat, Turkey, *Archéologie Islamique*, 5, 54–80.

Rodziewicz, M., 1976. *Alexandrie I: La céramique romaine tardive d'Alexandrie*, Warsaw: Editions scientifiques de Pologne.

Rodziewicz, M., 1978. *La céramique émaillée copte de Kom el Dikka*, *Études et Traveaux*, 10, 337–345.

Rodziewicz, M., 1983. Egyptian glazed pottery of the eighth to ninth centuries, *Bulletin de la société d'archéologie copte*, 25, 73–75.

Rogers, J. M., Ward, R. M., 1988. *Suleyman the Magnificent*, London: British Museum Publications.

Röhrs, S., Dumazet, A., Kuntz, K., and Franke, U., 2022. Bodies and Glazes of architectural ceramics from the Ilkhanid period at Takht-e Soleyman (North-Western Iran), *Minerals*, 12(158), 1–17.

Rooksby, H. P., 1964. A yellow cubic lead tin oxide opacifier in ancient glasses, *Physics and Chemistry of Glasses*, 5, 20–25.

Rottenborg, R., and Blanke, L., 2017. Jarash in the Islamic Ages (c. 700–1200 CE): A critical review, *Levant*, 40(3), 312–332.

Rugiadi, M., 2010. Processing Iranian Glazed Pottery of the Masjid-i Jum'a in Isfahan, in P. Matthiae, F. Pinnock, L. Nigro, and N. Marchetti (eds.), *Proceedings of the 6th International Congress of the Archaeology of the Ancient Near East*, 3, Wiesbaden: Harrassowitz, 173–190.

Rugiadi, M., 2011. The emergence of Siliceous-Paste in Iran in the last quarter of the 11th century and related issues: The dated assemblage from the Southern Domed Hall of the Great Mosque of Isfahan', *Proceedings of the 6th ICAANE Congress*, Rome, 5–10 May 2008, 'Sapienza' Universit. di Roma, Vicino & Medio Oriente XV, 233–248.

Rugiadi, M., 2016. Stonepaste Technology in Syria and Iran, in S. Canby, D. Beyazit, M. Rugiadi, and A. C. S. Peacock (eds.), *Court and Cosmos: The Great Age of the Seljuqs*. New Haven: Yale University Press, 179–187.

Sacco, V., 2017. Le ceramiche invetriatedi età islámica a Palermo; nuovi dati dalle sequenze del quartiere della Kalsa, *Archeol Mediev*, 49, 337–366.

Salinas, E., and Pradell, T., 2018. The transition from lead transparent to tin-opacifed productions in the western Islamic lands: al-Andalus, c. 875–929 CE, *Journal of Archaeological Science*, 45, 1–11.

Salinas, E., and Pradell, T., 2020. Madīnat al-Zahrā' or Madīnat Qurtuba? First evidences of the Caliphate tin glaze production of 'verde y manganeso' ware, *Archaeological and Anthropological Sciences*, 12, paper 207(19pgs).

Salinas, E., Pradell, T., Matin, M., and Tite, M. S., 2019. From tin- to antimony-based yellow opacifiers in the early Islamic Egyptian glazes: Regional influences and ruling dynasties, *Journal of Archaeological Sciences: Reports*, 29, 1–12.

Salinas, E., Reynolds, P., and Pradell, T., 2022. Technological changes in the glazed wares of northern Tunisia in the transition from Fatimid to Zirid rule, *Archaeological and Anthropological Sciences*, 14, 224–239.

Salinas, E., Reynolds, P., Tite, M. S., and Pradell, T., 2020. Polychrome glazed ware production in Tunisia during the Fatimid-Zirid period: New data on the question of the introduction of tin glazes in western Islamic lands, *Journal of Archaeological Sciences: Reports*, 34, 1026–1032.

Sauvaget, J., 1948. Tessons de Rakka, *Ars Islamica*, XIII–XIV, 31–45.

Sardar, M., 2015. NISHAPUR. vii. Excavations by the Metropolitan Museum of Art, *Encyclopædia Iranica*, online edition, www.iranicaonline.org/art icles/nishapur-07-met-excavations.

Sarre, F., 1925. *Die Keramik von Samarra*, Berlin: D. Reimer.

Sarre, F., 1930–31. The Seljuk and Early Osmanli Pottery of Miletus, *Transactions of the Oriental Ceramic Society* (1930–1931), 7, 20–23.

Scanlon, G. T., 1984. Mamluk pottery: More evidence from Fustat, *Muqarnas*, 2, 115–126.

Schibille, N., 2011. Late Byzantine mineral soda high alumina glasses from Asia Minor: A new primary glass production group, *PLoS ONE*, 6(4), e18970.

Sedighian, H., 2010. *Barresi Baastaanshenasi Sofaalhaay-e Eslami-e Mohavateh Moshkin Tepe Parandak*, Unpublished master's dissertation, University of Tehran [In Persian].

Shishkina, G. V., and Pavchinskaja, L. V., 1992. *Terres secrètes de Samarcande: Céramiques du VIIIe au XIIIe siècle*, Institut du Monde Arabe; Paris, 26 June-27 Septembre 1992; Musée de Normandie.

Siméon, P., 2012. Les ateliers de potiers en Asie centrale, entre Samarqand et Nishapur : approche critique, de la conquête musulmane au XIIe siècle, *Atti del IXCongresso Internazionale sulla Ceramica Medievale nel Mediterraneo*, Venice, 1, 15–21.

Siméon, P., 2017. Buff Ware Pottery: New Considerations; Typology, Chronology and Futuwwa Evidence, *Tribu, Jahbruch des Linden-Museums*, 66, 105–129.

Simsek, G., Unsalan, O., Bayraktar, K., Colomban, Ph., 2019, On-site pXRF analysis of glaze composition and colouring agents of "Iznik" tiles at Edirne mosques (15th and 16th-centuries), *Ceramics International*, 45(1), 595–605.

Smith, C. S., 1981. *A Search for Structure: Selected Essays on Science, Art and History*, Cambridge, MA: MIT Press.

Smith, D. T., 2006. Appendix 2: Compositional analysis of early-thirteenth-centruy ceramics from Raqqa and related sites, in M. Jenkins-Madina (ed.), *Raqqa Revisited: Ceramics of Ayyubid Syria*, New York: Metropolitan Museum of Art, 221–237.

Smithsonian Institute, Washington, DC; Arthur M. Sackler Gallery; National Heritage Board, Singapore; Singapore Tourism Board, 2011. *Shipwrecked, Tang treasures and monsoon winds*.

Soustiel, J., 1985. La céramique islamique : le guide du connaisseur, Fribourg: Office du Livre.

Tamari, V., 1995. Abbasid Blue-on-White Ware, in J. Allan (ed.), *Islamic Art in the Ashmolean Museum*, Part two, Oxford: Oxford University Press.

Testolini, V., 2018. Ceramic technology and cultural change in Sicily from the 6th to the 11th century AD. PhD thesis, University of Sheffield. https://doi.org/10.15131/shef.data.11567910.

Thiriot, J., 1997. Les fours pour la preparation des glacures dans le monde mediterraneen, in G. Demians d'Archimbaud (ed.), *La Céramique médiévale en Méditerranée. Actes du VIe Congrès de l'AIECM2. Aix-en-Provence (13-18 novembre 1995)*, Aix-en-Provence: Narration Editions, 513–522.

Ting, C., and Taxel, I., 2020. Indigeneity and innovation of early Islamic glaze technology, the case of the Coptic Glazed Ware, *Archaeological and Anthropological Sciences*, 12(27), 1–19.

Tite, M. S., 1988. Inter-relationship between Chinese and Islamic ceramics from 9th to 16th century A.D., in R. M. Farquhar, R. G. V. Hancock, and L. A. Pavlish (eds.), *Proceedings of the 26th International Archaeometry Symposium*, Archaeometry Laboratory, Department of Physics, University of Toronto, 30–34.

Tite, M. S., 1989. Iznik pottery: An investigation of the methods of production, *Archaeometry*, 31, 115–132.

Tite, M. S., 1991. Technological investigations of Italian Renaissance ceramics, in T. Wilson (ed.), *Italian Renaissance Pottery*, London: British Museum Press, 280–285.

Tite, M. S., 1992. The impact of electron microscopy on ceramic studies, in A. M. Pollard (ed.), *New Developments in Archaeological Science (Proceedings of the British Academy vol. 77)*. Oxford: Oxford University Press, 111–131.

Tite, M. S., 2009. The production technology of Italian maiolica: A reassesment, *Journal of Archaeological Science*, 36, 2065–2080.

Tite, M. S., and Maniatis, Y., 1975. Examination of Ancient pottery using the scanning electron microscope, *Nature*, 257, 122–123.

Tite, M. S., and Shortland, A. J., 2004. Report on the scientific examination of a glazed brick from Susa: Glazes, in T. Stoller, R. Slotta, and A. Vatandoust (eds.), *Persiens Antike Pracht – Band 2*, Bochum: Deutschen Bergbau-Museums Bochum, 388–390.

Tite, M. S., Freestone, I. C., Meeks, N., and Bimson, M., 1982. The use of scanning electron microscopy in the technological examination of ancient ceramics, in J. S. Olin and A. D. Franklin (eds.), *Archaeological Ceramics*, Washington, DC: Smithsonian Institution Press, 109–120.

Tite, M. S., Freestone, I., Mason, R. et al., 1998. Lead glazes in antiquity—methods of production and reasons for use, *Archaeometry*, 40, 241–260.

Tite, M. S., Freestone, I. C., and Bimson, M., 1983. Egyptian Faience: an investigation of the methods of production, *Archaeometry*, 25 (1), 17–27.

Tite, M. S., and Shortland, A. J., 2008, *Production Technology of Faience and Related early Vitreous Materials*, Oxford: Oxford University School of Archaeology, Monograph 72.

Tite, M. S., Watson, O., Pradell, T., et al. 2015. Revisiting the beginnings of tin-opacified Islamic glazes, *Journal of Archaeological Science*, 57, 80–91.

Tite, M. S., Shortland, A. J., Schibille, N., and Degryse, P., 2016. New data on the soda flux used in the production of Iznik glazes and Byzantine glasses, *Archaeometry*, 58, 57–67.

Tite, M. S., Wolf, S., and Mason, R. B., 2011. The technological development of stonepaste ceramics from the Islamic Middle East, *Journal of Archaeological Science*, 38(3), 570–580.

Tonghini, C., 1994. The Fine Wares of Ayyubid Syria, in E. J. Grube (ed.), *Cobalt and Lustre: The First Centuries of Islamic Pottery*, Oxford: Nour Foundation, 249–294.

Tonghini, C., 1995. A new Islamic pottery sequence in Syria: Tell Shahin, *Levant*, **XXVII**, 197–207.

Tonghini, C., 1998. *Qal'at Jabar Pottery: A Study of a Syrian Fortified Site in the Late 11th-14th Centuries*, Council for British Research in the Levant (CBRL), Oxford: Oxford University Press.

Turner, W. E. S., and Rooksby, H. P., 1961. Further historical studies based on X-ray diffraction methods of the reagents employed in making opal and opaque glasses, *Jahrbuch des Römisch-Germanischen Zentralmuseum*, 8, 1–6.

Vendrell, M., Molera, J., and Tite, M. S., 2007. Optical properties of tin-opacified glazes, *Archaeometry*, 42(2), 325–340.

Vorderstrasse, T., 2005. *Al-Mina: A Port of Antioch from Late Antiquity to the End of the Ottomans*, Leiden: Nederlands Instituut voor het Nabije Oosten.

Waagé, F. O., 1948. *Antioch-on-the-Orontes IV, Part One: Ceramics and Islamic Coins*, Princeton: Princeton University Press.

Walmsley, A., 2001. Turning east: The appearance of Islamic cream wares in Jordan, the end of antiquity? in E. Villeneuve and P. M. Watson (eds.), *La Céramique Byzantine et Proto-Islamique en Syrie-Jordanie (IVe-VIIIe siècles apr. J.-C.) Actes du Colloque tenu à Amman les 3,4 et 5 décembre 1994*, Beirut: Institut Français d'Archéologie du Proche Orient, 305–313.

Walmsley, A., 2007. *Early Islamic Syria: An Archaeological Assessment*, London: Duckworth.

Walton, M. S. and Tite, M. S., 2010. Production technology of Roman lead glazed pottery and its continuance into late antiquity, *Archaeometry*, 52, 733–759.

Watson, O., 1976. Persian Lustre-painted Pottery: The Rayy and Kashan Styles, *Transactions of the Oriental Ceramic Society*, XL, 1–20.

Watson, O., 1985a. *Persian Lustre Ware*, London: Faber and Faber.

Watson, O., 1985b. Fakes and Forgeries of Islamic Pottery, *The V&A Album*, 4, 38–46.

Watson, O., 1987. Islamic pots in Chinese style, *The Burlington Magazine*, 129 (1010), 304–206.

Watson, O., 1994. Documentary Mina'i and Abu Zaid's Bowls', in R. Hillenbrand (ed.), *The Art of the Saljuqs in Iran and Anatolia*, Costa Mesa: Mazda, 170–180.

Watson, O., 1999a. Fritware: Fatimid Egypt or Saljuq Iran? in M. Barrucand (ed.), *L'Egypte Fatimide; son art et son histoire*, Paris: Universite de Paris-Sorbonne, 299–310.

Watson, O., 1999b. VIII. Report on the Glazed Ceramics, in P. A. Miglus (ed.), *Ar-Raqqa I: Die Frühislamische Keramik von Tell Aswad, Mainz*, 81–87, Taf. 94–99.

Watson, O., 2004. *Ceramics from Islamic Lands*, London: Thames and Hudson.

Watson, O., 2014. Revisiting Samarra: The rise of Islamic glazed pottery, in J. Gonnella, R. Abdellatif and S. Struth (eds.), *Beiträge zur Islamischen Kunst und Archäologie*, Wiesbaden: Ludwig Reichert, 4, 125–144.

Watson, O., 2015. Pottery and Light, in Sh. Blair and J. Bloom (eds.), *God is the Light of Heavens and the Earth: Light in Islamic Art and Architecture, Biennial Hamad Bin Khalifa Symposium on Islamic Art and Culture (5th, 2013, Palermo, Italy)*, New Haven: Yale University Press in association with Qatar Foundation, Virginia Commonwealth University, and Virginia Commonwealth University School of the Arts in Qatar, 157–175.

Watson, O., 2020. *Ceramics of Iran: Islamic Pottery from Sarikhani Collection*, London: Yale University Press.

Watson, O., 2024. Mina'i from Fustat: An Iranian Spoke in a Fatimid Ceramic Wheel, Sheila S. Blair, Jonathan M. Bloom, and Sandra Williams (eds), *Iranian Art from the Sassanians to the Islamic Republic, Essays in Honour of Linda Komaroff*, Edinburgh: Edinburgh University Press, 239–248.

Watt, J. C. Y., 1979. Notes on the use of cobalt in later Chinese ceramics, *Ars Orientalis*, 11, 63–85.

Wen, R., 2012. *The Cobalt Blue Pigment Used on Islamic Ceramics and Chinese Blue-and-white Porcelain*, unpublished DPhil dissertation, University of Oxford.

Wen, W., 2018. *Chinese ceramics in the Islamic World from the 8th to 10th centuries CE*, Unpublished DPhil thesis, University of Oxford.

Wen, R., and Pollard, M., 2014. The pigments applied to Islamic mina'i wares and the correlation with Chinese blue-and-white porcelain, *Archaeometry*, **58** (1), 1–16.

Weyl, W. A., 1951. *Coloured Glasses: Society of Glass Technology.* London: Dawson.

Wickham, C., 2023. *The Donkey and the Boat: Reinterpreting the Mediterranean Economy*, Oxford: Oxford University Press, 950–1180.

Whitcomb, D., 1989. Glazed ceramics from the excavations at Aqaba, Jordan, *Journal of the American Research Centre in Egypt*, 26, 167–182.

Whitcomb, D., 1991. Glazed ceramics of the Abbasid period from the Aqaba excavations, *Transactions of the Oriental Ceramic Society (1990-91)*, 55, 43–65.

Whitcomb, D., 1999. Hadir Qinnasrin, The Oriental Institute of the University of Chicago, 1998-1999 Annual Report, 76–83.

Whitehouse, D., 1979. Islamic Glazed Pottery in Iraq and the Persian Gulf: The ninth and tenth centuries, *Annali dell'Instituto Orientale di Napoli*, 39, 45–61.

Whitehouse, D., 1978. The origins of Italian maiolica, *Archaeology*, 31, 42–49.

Whitehouse, D., 1972. Excavations at Siraf, Fifth Interim Report, *IRAN*, 10, 63–87.

Wilkinson, C. K., 1947. Fashion and Technique in Persian Pottery, *The Metropolitan Museum of Art Bulletin*, 6(3), 99–104.

Wilkinson, C. K., 1959. The Kilns of Nishapur, *The Metropolitan Museum of Art Bulletin*, New Series, 17(9), 235–240.

Wilkinson, C. K., 1973. *Nishapur: Pottery of the Early Islamic Period*, New York: The Metropolitan Museum of Art Bulletin.

Williamson, A. G., 1971. Regional distribution of medieval Persian pottery in the light of recent investigations, in J. Allan and C. Roberts (eds.), *Syria and Iran: Three Studies in Medieval Ceramics*, Oxford: Oxford University Press, 11–22.

Wood, N., Doherty, C., and Rosser-Owen, M., 2009. A technological study of Iraqi copies of Chinese Changsha and Chinese Sancai wares found at Samarra–together with some Chinese originals, Gu Taoci Kexue Jishu, 8, 154–180.

Wright, H., 1984. Early Seafarers of the Comoro Islands: The Dembeni Phase of the IXth-Xth Centuries A.D., Azania, 19, 13–59.

Wulff, H. E., 1966. The Traditional Crafts of Persia, Cambridge, MA: MIT Press.

Cambridge Elements ☰

Archaeological Perspectives on Materials and Technologies

A. Mark Pollard
University of Oxford

A. Mark Pollard is Emeritus Professor of Archaeological Science at the University of Oxford. His publications include *Beyond Provenance: New Approaches to Interpreting the Chemistry of Archaeological Copper Alloys* (University of Leuven Press, 2018), *Archaeological Chemistry* (Royal Society of Chemistry, 2017), and *Handbook of Archaeological Sciences* (Wiley, 2001).

Chris Gosden
University of Oxford

Chris Gosden is Professor of European Archaeology at the University of Oxford, and his publications include *Celtic Art in Europe: Making Connections* (2014), *A Technology of Enchantment? Exploring Celtic Art 400 BC – AD 100* (2012) and *Archaeology and Colonialism* (2004).

Editorial Board

About the Series

Examining technology on a worldwide basis from the earliest human use of tools to the early modern period, this series focuses on new archaeological findings, and integrates these with historical textual sources where they exist. It considers how things were done, why they were done that way, and how an understanding of the world was generated through making and using materials.

Cambridge Elements ☰

Archaeological Perspectives on Materials and Technologies

Printed in the United States
by Baker & Taylor Publisher Services